Seasons
Depression. Pregnancy. Motherhood.

Maria Koval

Copyright © 2024 Maria Koval

All rights reserved. No part of this book may be reproduced or transmitted in any form or by any means, electronic or mechanical, including photocopying, recording or by any information storage and retrieval system without permission in writing from the publisher.

Matstepkoff Press—Brooklyn, NY
ISBN: 979-8-218-49096-6
Library of Congress Control Number: 2024920787
Title: *Seasons: Depression. Pregnancy. Motherhood.*
Author: Maria Koval
Digital distribution | 2024
Paperback | 2024

Dedication

To my children:

Please be patient. Be patient with me. While I learn you. While I learn to care for you. While I learn the new me. While I learn to love you. Please be patient with me, when I make mistakes, when I try my best.

Please forgive me. Forgive me for my shortcomings. Forgive me for my awkward journey to becoming your mother. Forgive me while I give myself time to adjust to the new reality, new life, new me, with you. The journey is long, but it's amazing. It's already amazing, but it's going to become even more eventful, even more beautiful.

Chapter One
The Before

I was on the train, minding my own business, as I usually do. I was on my way to work. It was an early morning. Something was off. I could feel the coldness inside of me. I was glancing at people around, watching them closely. One girl was reading a book called "*Nothing General about It*" by Maurice Benard. I haven't read it, but I took note of it. I thought to myself, "I wonder if this girl is really into the book, or is she thinking about something else?" I bet if people on this train were watching me, I would give out this "thinker" type of vibe. I turned my head to the right and another girl was putting on makeup. Just casually putting on a full face of makeup on the train. I salute her for this. I realize it could be a long ride, but the shakiness and all the people around would never allow me to be comfortable enough to put a full face of makeup on the train. It is very challenging. I'm too self-conscious.

I heard a loudspeaker come on and the train crew said, I bet, something very important, but as usual, it was impossible to hear. I just hoped that it wasn't an announcement about skipping my stop. I was supposed to get off at the Atlantic Ave - Barclays Center. Just a couple more stops to go. I laid my eyes on a man in dark blue sneakers. He was holding a black backpack in his hand and kind of sleeping. He was sleeping standing up. I thought to myself, "He must be so exhausted." While I was watching people on this train, I knew exactly what I was doing. I wasn't just watching for fun, I was escaping. I was destructing myself. I was destructing myself from my thoughts.

I am usually a very self-aware person. I recognize the patterns that I sometimes do. I was watching people; it allowed me to imagine different lives, different scenarios, different struggles and challenges that these people might be going through. It destructs me from my own life, my own thoughts. It's a coping mechanism that I picked up when I was a teenager, maybe even earlier in life. I don't know exactly when it happened, but I destruct myself a lot, in different ways. Watching people and imagining their lives is just one of the ways. It seems easier, it seems calmer to destruct myself, because who wants to face struggles head-on? Not me.

Throughout years, I learned that it's important to feel these difficulties of life. To feel pain, to absorb the struggles. I'm not the best at it, I'm actually the worst. I run from anything that makes me feel anxious. I run from anything that makes me mad, angry, or sad. I run figuratively, but also quite literally. It's easier to just walk away, run away, forget about it. Walk away from the fight, walk away from an unpleasant situation, smooth the corners by "apologizing." Yes, a lot of people pleasing was going on in my life. I am this way. Walk away from sadness. Unfortunately, I learned that I can't always walk away. I can't keep hiding from my life. There is no walking away from yourself. I realized it only when I was closer to 30 years old. I have reached a point in my life where I finally said, "enough is enough," I got tired of running.

Frankly, I got tired of running emotionally, because for the life of me I would never run for real. I got tired of constantly trying to avoid anything that makes me upset. I got so tired. Every time there would be some sort of argument, my initial reaction is to walk away, to storm out, to run. I would walk in the unknown direction, for as long as I want. I got tired of escaping, because you can only do so for so long. My emotions got the best of me, and I fell. Metaphorically.

I was just minding my own business, as I usually do. Days went by, weeks went by, my days consisted of me going to and from work. There wasn't much else. Days were just passing by, passing through. I had no sense of time. Time just got away from me. I constantly felt like I was always late getting somewhere, even though there was nowhere to be. This feeling of "lateness" made me feel very exhausted, because I hate being late. This time, I didn't even know where I'm being late to. I was running to the train, I was running home, I was running to get lunch; I was just constantly running somewhere. I had no idea where I'm running. What is my final destination? Sitting on the train and watching people was my only time where I didn't have to run. I had nothing to do, so I had to stop and wait until my stop. I started noticing some changes within me. It sneaks up on you. I started noticing my carelessness. One time, back in the day I already felt it. I was familiar with this feeling of emptiness. Complete carelessness, no reason for anything. I got scared.

"This can't be happening, I'm healed. I'm okay. I can't feel this."

Last time I had this feeling of numbness was when I was going to college, trying to get my life together, figure out what I want to do. Very confusing time of my life. I thought college was my future, my way to go, but life had other plans. I coped with my feelings by sleeping. I remember coming home from college and just crashing on my bed. I took a three - four-hour nap, and then just watched some TV shows. That was my escape. It was years and years after that when I realized that I was suffering from depression.

All those emotions came back to me, but this time, it was more, it was intensified. It was more serious. I was scared. I didn't know what to do. I didn't know how to deal with it. For the first time in my life, I actually thought about seeing a psychiatrist. I was always afraid of pills. I was always thinking about the stigma that surrounds pills and psychiatrists. I was so judgmental towards myself. I judge myself pretty harshly, so when I actually accepted the fact that I need help, I was pretty surprised. I had no other way out. I didn't see a way out of this by myself. As days went by, I contemplated seeing a doctor. I still had hope that I can deal with this. I had a strong belief that maybe it's going to go away on its own. Maybe, just maybe, I can heal once again without outside help. I had hope that it was just a temporary setback. Maybe because it's Monday, maybe because it's raining, maybe it's my period coming, maybe because it's still cold in May. I was so hopeful that it wasn't a real depression. I was in such disbelief. I only thought about the seriousness of the situation when it was hard for me to contain my tears. Tears are how our bodies tell us that we need mental rest. I heard somewhere that if your nose is runny, it means your body is showing you that you need physical rest. I even stopped wearing makeup, because tears would just run down my cheeks without my control. Without any reason. It felt good to let it out, but at the same time, it was scary.

I came to realization that I need help. A big part of it came from working at a psychiatric office. So many people, so many stories, so many lives. When I first started working there, I was full of energy, and positivity. As time went on, I understood that working with people is not for everyone. It's only good for a couple of months. My energy went drastically down, and my patience disappeared. One day, I met a patient, she was in her twenties. While I was checking her in, we got to talking and I felt like this girl was so vulnerable, was so alone. She told me the story how she lost her mom to breast cancer. Tragic. But that wasn't the end of her suffering. After her mom's passing, her father committed suicide by hanging, she found him. I cannot even begin to imagine the sorrow; she must be feeling. She was in desperate need of help. I am an empath by nature, so I kind of held her pain in my heart. The heaviness that she must be feeling, the loneliness, the despair, sadness.... I cannot even imagine, but at the same time, it was almost like I could. This girl was coming in for her sessions once per week to see a therapist, and once per month to see a psychiatrist. We became good acquaintances. This girl actually showed me that you can only be broken if you can be broken. Read that again. As human beings, we were made to surpass all obstacles. We are the strongest creatures on Earth, mentally. Yes, sometimes we need help, yes, sometimes it seems like we can't do it, but we can. Nothing is concrete. Nothing is set in stone. Unless it is. Only death can stop us. Even that is not for sure. This encounter of mine, led me to realize that every person is struggling with something. Big or small. The fact that our schedule for therapists and psychiatrists had a month-long waiting list, says a lot. Witnessing this, and feeling the way I was feeling, I finally decided to get myself help. To accept that I need help. It was a big step for me. The step that I had to take to be better.

***

For a while, I felt like my life was just passing by. Like it wasn't my life at all. I was a guest in my own life. It was all a dream. The exhaustion, the sadness, the emptiness that I felt inside, felt unreal. Hours were passing by, days, weeks, and I felt like I wasn't even living it. This life, this routine was killing me. At first, I thought it was just a bad day, just a couple of bad days, but then it was all there was. Bad days. I was living through it over and over. I was trying to cheer myself up, but nothing worked. It was bigger than me. These feelings scared me because it was all so familiar. These feelings of sadness, these feelings of infinite hopelessness, this black hole inside of me.

Not being able to feel anything. My thoughts flooded with the unknown.

"How do I get out of this? What should I do?"

I was trying to find a solution, but the only reasonable and logical answer that I could come up with was to go see a psychiatrist. I thought I was fine, not good, but fine. I thought it's going to resolve on its own, but as time went on, I found myself on the ground, not able to get up, think, or do anything. I was sinking deeper and deeper into the unknown.

I was 30 years old when I finally accepted that I need help. That's the first step. I need to see a doctor, a professional, a psychiatrist. I was at the point where I couldn't handle myself, emotionally. I was drowning in tears and my own unpleasant thoughts. I say unpleasant, but these thoughts that I had were actually devastating. My thoughts were dark. Very dark. My thoughts felt like they weren't even mine. It was almost like someone else was in my head. I couldn't believe it. I was trying to rationalize everything, I was trying to think clearly, but nothing was working. I was thinking that I'm a burden to everyone in my life. I was thinking that I was all alone. I was thinking horrible things about myself, and I couldn't stop it. I couldn't stop it even when I really wanted to.

Unfortunately, people don't understand what depression is. You can't see it. You can't even fully describe it. You can't prove it. Usually, people will try to cheer you up, make silly jokes, maybe tickle you a little, and constantly ask how you are doing. And so you play along, you smile and nod your head, and laugh at the silly jokes, and try to make a decent conversation. But the problem is not that you feel a little sad, and can't take a joke or you can't laugh at the joke, the problem is that you have no energy at all. While depressed, you can smile, and laugh and act like nothing happened, but it takes up all of your energy. It takes up the energy that you don't even have. You feel completely drained. You feel empty inside. You feel lost. You feel numb to all of the emotions that a person is supposed to feel. I had this weird careless posture, I couldn't even get mad at anything, I was completely numb.

I was spacing out a lot, during a conversation, or just in general. I was in my head, but at the same time not there at all. I was feeling depressed. I was depressed, but I was so afraid to acknowledge it, because, once again, the unknown. I was so afraid to become a burden, a person around which people will have to walk on eggshells. At the same time, I wanted for someone to know, I wanted for someone to help me. I needed that hand of hope, a ray of sunshine. A lot of people think that depression has to be caused by something, an event, or life obstacles. While it can be true, it's not always the case. Nothing has to happen. Depression is caused by the imbalance of brain chemicals. That's why it's difficult to understand depression. I did not tell my husband about my depression, because I was not ready for the "cheering me up" conversation. It's not because he wouldn't understand, it was just my way of dealing with it. I wanted to do it on my own. I wanted to get out of it without anyone worrying about me. I acted like nothing is happening. Just bad mood swings, bad weather, bad day, bad week....

I was struggling alone. Depression is lonely, it's isolating. At first, I thought I have it under control, but when shopping didn't help, I started to get worried. My loneliest times were actually in the most crowded spaces, on the train. As much as I hated the New York City subway, I kind of felt fascinated by it. My eyes were seeing all kinds of people, but at the same time, I was all alone. I felt so lonely on the train. "I'm all alone with my thoughts, my problems, my feelings, nobody knows about it."

Depression is lonely. I know that I wasn't the only one suffering from this disease, but at that time, it felt like it. It was devastating. "Maybe, just maybe, I will take the magical pills, and I will get back to normal? To myself? Or maybe, I will find a new version of me, a completely different version that is depression-free?" I was thinking to myself, trying to further convince myself to see a psychiatrist. "What if there is another person inside of me? What if I haven't even met her yet? A person who will enjoy life, who has all the energy in the world to do what makes her happy? But what makes me happy?"

I had no idea. At this time, I have already scheduled my appointment with the psychiatrist. I didn't want to see a psychiatrist in my office, because I didn't want my dirty laundry at the place where I work, so I found another doctor. I was so nervous, I wrote all my symptoms on a piece of paper, so I wouldn't forget. I waited for this appointment patiently, and was yet so jittery.

Depression and anxiety are tied together. I had very high levels of anxiety. My cuticle biting and leg shaking was out of control. I was also biting my lips, and not at all in a sexy way, I was playing with my hair. These are all symptoms of high functioning anxiety and soothing techniques. I was anxious all the time about everything, but at the same time there was no reason for me to be anxious, I was over-thinking. I had intrusive thoughts, something like, "What if my jacket gets caught in the train doors and I will be dragged by the train and killed."

All kinds of scary thoughts. It was at that time when I learned a saying: will cross that bridge when we get there. It actually helped me a lot. What is the point of worrying about something if it hasn't even happened yet? That's the problem with the anxiety, it's irrational.

One time my anxiety got the best of me. It was early spring. The weather was shitty. It was windy and raining. As usual, I didn't want to go to work, but it was a workday and taking a sick day wasn't an option. If I could, I would, trust me. I'm all for using all your sick and personal days, because I value my life, which is not my job. I have a job simply to pay my bills and afford the little things that I sometimes crave. I was running late, but due to my personal emotional state, I did not care. I was depressed and officially accepting it. I went into a train station, like I did every single day, and heard my usual train departing. Was I upset? Hell no. I refilled my MetroCard, slowly, and proceeded to head to the platform. I found a spot on the bench and sat down. I was listening to rain. Droplets were sliding down the platform. I love rain. I love it even more when I don't need to be anywhere. Imagine, waking up when you want, listening to the rain outside, and you just cozied up in your bed; then you go to the kitchen and make yourself a cup of coffee, and you sit and enjoy, staring out of the window, looking at the people who are actually going to work. Oh... what a beautiful way to start the day. This was not it; I was sitting on the train station. Pigeons were murmuring something, at the same time shitting all over the place.

"Is it going to be a good day?" I thought to myself. I had no idea.

My train came and I departed. It was a relatively short ride to Atlantic Ave – Barclays Center, about 20 minutes or so. As I always do, I watched people, it was also because of my anxiety. I try to see and remember the people who were with me on the train, because what if something goes wrong, and I have to remember who was there. I don't know, the mind works in mysterious ways. Half way through my travel time, the train stopped. It happens, I didn't think much of it. Usually, it's for a couple of minutes. A couple minutes passed, but we weren't moving, nothing was happening, nothing was advised by the train crew. I was curious. More time passed, and a loud speaker came on, "We will be moving momentarily."

Another 10 minutes passed, but we weren't moving still. I have a bit of claustrophobia, so I was already starting to feel the pressure. I was underground, in a closed train wagon, cell service was on and off. I was officially very late to work.

In general, I prefer ground transportation; car would be my first choice, then would be the bus. I feel safer for some reason. I can see through the window, I can get off on any stop, it's just a different vibe. Airplane would be my last choice. I hate flying. Trains kind of freak me out and now I actually have a reason. We finally started moving. I texted my boss the situation, there was nothing I could do. We stopped at the next stop and the train conductor announced that no trains will be running any further and everybody should get off and out of the train station and take the shuttle bus. It wasn't my stop. I got off the train and saw a lot of police officers patrolling the station. I had a little tremor in my heart, but I got out of the train station and followed the crowd to the shuttle bus stop. I had no idea what was going on.

I was walking with all the people from the train, towards the bus stop. It was raining, and I, for some reason, didn't have an umbrella. Actually, the reason is simple. I always lose my umbrellas, so what's the point of taking an umbrella if I'm going to lose it anyway. I was already getting pissed off at the fact that my feet were starting to get wet. I was walking and thinking that MTA fucked up again. All of a sudden, I hear a loud noise above. I look up and see a helicopter. Then I see another one. They were circling around, looking to pick me up. Of course, I'm joking, but they surely were looking for something, or someone. I officially started to freak out. Rain was pouring harder, people were running somewhere, the whole atmosphere was giving me chills. I finally thought of Googling what was happening.

Headlines screamed, "New York City Subway attack."

"A mass shooting was committed on a northbound N train…"

I said to myself out loud, "Oh my God!"

But after a minute or so, I realized that it happened on my usual train that I was late for. I stopped walking. I took a breath. I called my husband. People were walking by, talking about this whole situation. My mind automatically went into a survival mode. I didn't even know it was happening. I was not panicking, or worrying too much. I went into a survival mode, where I had to be okay. I had to make sure that I'm okay. I waited for the shuttle bus, but all those buses were passing by were full of people. No buses stopped to pick us up. I decided to walk. I walked and walked under the rain, officially soaked. There was nothing I could do. I wanted to go to the bathroom because I had my second cup of coffee, so I stopped at some playground and checked if the bathroom was open, to my surprise it was. So that was taken care of. I honestly had no thoughts, or feelings at that point, I was just trying to get to work. I was just trying to get somewhere, either home or work, but no trains were running in neither direction. By foot, it was another 40 minutes or so to get to my office. There was so much traffic. People were panicking. Police cars, helicopters, all force of New York were going towards the crime scene. In these extreme situations, I could see how powerful my city is. I love New York. It might sound crazy that I declare my love for my city in this situation, but I have lived here for so long, I got used to it. Not the rats, not the constantly late MTA, not the homeless people can turn me away from my city. Any city has its own flaws, but it might as well be this grand, beautiful, one-of-a-kind – New York.

I stopped at the grocery store to get some coffee, or something, because I had to think about my next steps. I honestly have never seen so much traffic. I've never been in such extreme circumstances. I called my boss to explain the situation, and he suggested he get me a car so I should stay where I'm currently at. My cab arrived in like 25 minutes, through the traffic and everything. It was another 40 minutes to get to my job, maneuvering through this chaos. While I was in the car, I was a bit shaken. News already traveled to my relatives and my friends, so people started texting and calling me, asking if I am okay. I finally got to my office, I was 3 ½ late, but does it even matter in this situation? I was all wet and wanted to go to the bathroom. I was totally fine. I did my business, washed my hands, but when I came out…iIt happened. My very first panic attack.

All of a sudden, the office got dark. It was almost like I lost my sight. I couldn't even get to my desk. I carefully slid down on the floor, and was just trying to catch my breath. Nothing was working. I was trying to count, I was trying to tap my fingers together, I was trying to calm down. Nothing was working. All kinds of breathing techniques. I was spiraling out of control. My heart felt like it's going to jump out of my chest. My palms got really sweaty; I had heavy, irregular breathing. I couldn't comprehend what was happening to me. My whole body started shaking, and I couldn't stop crying. At one point, I thought that this is what the end looks like. I thought I was dying. My boss saw me in this state and helped me get to the back office. Thankfully, it's a psychiatric clinic, so he consulted one of our doctors and offered me half of a pill of a sedative. He brought me water, and asked if I could call someone to talk to me. I don't remember much of who I called, and what we talked about, but I know that I should've called my therapist. I was not thinking clearly. Half of that pill did not work for me, so he gave me the second half. I was not okay; I was scared for my life. My temples were throbbing, I thought that I am seriously dying, on this chair in this office. That's not how I wanted to go, but I guess we can't choose right? After I sat in the dark room for about an hour, I was finally able to somewhat collect my thoughts. I sat at my desk, but it was all like a dream. I felt like my body was floating above my desk, and the computer. I bet it was the pill. The feeling was surreal. I was finally calm though, so I guess that's good. I don't remember how I worked the rest of the day, but I know that one patient came in and we had a good laugh. My husband came to pick me up at the end of the day, and I finally felt safe. I sat in the back of his car, and cried on the way home. The rest of the day was such a blur.

The next day I was supposed to go to work, again. It's crazy how we need to go to work every day, I don't appreciate it. Was I going to take the train? No. Thankfully I had a car. For those who are not familiar with New York, taking a car to Downtown Brooklyn, is not the best idea. There is usually a lot of traffic, and you can seriously forget about parking. There is no parking. No street parking or any other parking options, except for garages, but even those get crowded very fast, and you are not guaranteed a spot. That did not stop me, because after what I have been through, I wasn't going to step foot on the train. After this incident, I was driving to and from work. It took longer, and it took extra money to park my car, but the experience of a panic attack was worse.

After this incident, I remember having nightmares. I used to wake up in the middle of the night in cold sweat and just trying to process everything. Trying to realize that I'm still alive and I'm okay. I was thinking to myself: "What if I wasn't late that morning? What if I was in the same wagon as the shooter? What if… What if…" I was devastated. My intrusive thoughts were blooming. I was coming up with crazy scenarios every day. Is this considered PTSD? After a while it dialed down, and I was okay, I don't think about it often, or actually, ever. That was definitely a scary experience.

***

My depression did not go away, but it was disguised. Something pulled me out of this misery, the only thing that was left was my anxiety, or so I thought. The adrenaline was so strong that I was floating on top of the waters again. Usually, I would've thought that I'm "healed" and cancelled the psychiatrist appointment, but not this time. This time I've decided to stay afloat.

Appointment was fast approaching and I was nervous. I was nervous for two reasons: I was afraid to get "hooked" on pills and to rely on pills for everything. And second, I was afraid to not explain myself correctly, and be misunderstood. Or judged? I wrote down all my symptoms, I even went and "diagnosed" myself through google, as well as DSM

5. Which is a Diagnostic and Statistical Manual of Mental Disorders. I have this book; I have actually read it. I guess you can say that my "little hobby" is diagnosing myself with all sorts of mental disorders. What I should've remembered is that not everything is a symptom, and not everything needs to have a diagnosis. Thinking about my upcoming appointment, I was nervous to come off a certain way. I was thinking about this appointment. It wasn't just a regular "Tuesday," this appointment meant a lot to me.

When I came face-to-face with depression, I was fascinated by this magical disease. Why is it magical? Because it's invisible. There is no way to prove it, there is no way to see it. I saw drastic changes in myself, like, inside of me, inside my mind, but physically too. Every time I go outside to work, or the store, or anywhere, for that matter, it feels like such an accomplishment. It feels like I'm doing something extraordinary. I feel so tired after every little thing. Going to the shower is a struggle. Putting on pants feels like such a task. Even opening my eyes in the morning feels like I'm ready to be done with the day. Waking up is hard. It's hard to hold my head straight, not literally. Sometimes it's hard to put together words into sentences. It's challenging to do the simple everyday life tasks. It's hard, but also, it feels so unnecessary. It seems like everything has no purpose, no meaning behind it. All the daily activities are just useless.

One time, I was standing in my kitchen, washing dishes. We didn't have a dishwasher, it was an old, dusty building in Brooklyn. I was doing it so automatically. I honestly did not even realize that I'm washing the dishes. I thought to myself, "Where is that pot that I recently cooked in?"

Turned out that I just washed it a couple of minutes ago, without even realizing it. I didn't remember doing it. Then my thoughts scattered, and I thought, "Why do we always have to wash the dishes? Why do we have this weird urge to clean? Why do we need to shower every day?"

At that point, I seriously was asking myself these questions. In my "normal" state, I understand the simple hygiene of the house, and self. I understand that washing the dishes, laundry, vacuuming, is to keep your environment clean, and to have a peace of mind, and to avoid roaches of course. I understand that taking a shower is very beneficial, not only for me, but for the people surrounding me as well. In my depressed episode, I wasn't comprehending these simple things.

I hated this feeling. I hated the feeling of constantly being tired. I hated myself for being "lazy." All my life, I just thought I'm extremely lazy, but as time went on, I saw my mental state affecting my "laziness." I wasn't lazy, I was depressed. I felt guilty for not telling my husband what is going on with me, and then I felt guilty for feeling guilty. Not opening up to my husband was hard, but I didn't want to be a burden. I didn't want to worry him with my problems. I didn't want him to worry about me. Depression is isolating. Depression is a loner. Depression is a bitch.

When I got to the point of being so scared for myself, I couldn't wait to take a pill. My appointment was finally here. I scheduled it after work, so I could sit in the park nearby, and just talk to the doctor, with no interruptions. It was a virtual appointment. The doctor was about 20 minutes late, I was getting frustrated, but I knew it was normal. When I finally saw him on the screen, I got shy and nervous. It's not every day I tell someone how I truly feel. He greeted me with the warmest smile and introduced himself. I started mumbling something and he asked me to speak up because he was having trouble hearing me. I had to adjust my voice volume. I thought to myself, "That's great, let me scream in this public park about my depression."

Immediately, I thought this was my fault, because I did not choose the best spot for this appointment, or I did not adjust my headphones, it was all my fault. With depression and anxiety comes great self-doubt. I constantly thought that everything is my fault, and I always apologized, for no reason at all. I wrote a list of my symptoms, and I asked him if I could read it to him. My list was broken down into three categories: depression symptoms, anxiety symptoms, and a couple more mental illnesses that I thought I had.

"Wow! Slow Down! Do you have a degree in Mental Health? Social Work? Psychology?"

"Not really," I answered.

"Let's refrain from unnecessary diagnosis, let's just agree that I call the shots in this appointment," he said it with a slight smile on his face, very calmly, but very confident.

He suggested that we tackle my anxiety first. He explained that sometimes when you take care of your anxiety, depression lessens because those two are sisters. He prescribed me medication for anxiety.

After the appointment, I was a bit shocked, because I thought I needed saving right away. I thought that my depression got so out of hand that I needed immediate intervention. I thought…. I thought…. I thought a lot. I thought that my depression symptoms were so severe, and they were, but psychiatry works by elimination. You try one medication, see how you feel, and then have another appointment with your doctor to discuss your findings and observations. Then you go from there.

Analyzing my depression, I became very self-aware. I know I'm not worthless, I do not want to hurt myself or others, I just want to sleep. My depression is very silent and very slow. Just like me sometimes. Well, it feels like that. Sometimes it whispers to me, "Let's not go to work" or "Let's have a drink" or "Let's not do anything." Let's be clear, nobody is talking to me, I am not hallucinating, it's just subtle thoughts that sometimes pop up. I just really want to sleep. Every moment of me being awake, every second of my day, I think about sleeping. The funny thing is that I don't think I physically can be unconscious for this long. I can't sleep this much.

Like the best patient that I am, I was taking the pills that were prescribed to me. Every single morning and evening, I was taking the medication in hopes to see the results. I had this light at the end of the tunnel, I was so hopeful. A week passed by, and I was looking for signs of improvement, but there were none. Nothing was happening. I was the same sad and lonely person inside. Two weeks passed by, but still nothing. It felt unreal, everything, going to work, coming back from work. Where did the time go? I didn't notice it; I didn't appreciate it. I used to do nothing and everything at the same time and my day was longer, it's like my life was longer. Now, I wake up, blink and half of the day is gone, and I will never get it back. Has it always been like that? I'm constantly being late. Not literally, mentally. This is what I feel like inside. I feel like I'm being late all the time and it frustrates me, because I hate being late. I'm exhausted. My anxiety is through the roof, because I always feel like I'm failing. Me, a person who is low key perfectionist, who is never late, who likes my life the way it is, at peace, always. I was confused. Time just got away from me and I can't control it. When I can't control something, I feel out of my element. Control is the only thing that keeps me sane. Just a little bit of control of the situation... I lose myself, I feel vulnerable. The irony of life is amazing though. You think you are headed in one direction, but then your life turns one-eighty. Usually, it's unexpected, and it's an adjustment, but everything comes when it's supposed to. Everything has its meaning and reason. My life's plot twist couldn't come at a better time.

***

Depression is lonely. I felt so isolated. I didn't have the energy to explain anything to anybody. Most importantly, I didn't want to be a burden. I didn't want for people to look at me differently. I didn't want them to think that I'm dying. Even though, it felt like I was dying inside. Deep, deep, somewhere inside, I wanted for someone to "save me," but only I, myself could've done that. I was so consumed by my depression, by my dark thoughts, that I didn't see a way out. It was all dark, all the time. Everywhere I went, I was left alone with my thoughts, by myself. There wasn't a day where I would see anything positive. Which was so unusual for me, because I'm generally a positive person. I used to see good things in everything, in my everyday life. I was shocked to realize that I'm not the same. I'm not that funny and joyful girl that I was. Everything was off. I didn't recognize myself, so what would be my expectation of people surrounding me? There were none. I didn't want to be a burden. This thought of mine was harassing me. "I don't want to be a burden for anybody, including myself."

The funny part about depression is actually when you get out of it. First of all, I was having trouble remembering myself while I was suffering from depression. Once I was out of the woods, looking back at everything, seemed like everything happened to someone else, not to me. It was like I was a very close witness in someone else's life. Second of all, I was very surprised at some of the changes that I went through while depressed. I wasn't exactly taking care of myself. I wasn't paying attention to what I eat, and what I do, therefore I gained weight. I wasn't watching what I ate, I mostly always wanted junk food, something greasy, something that would fill in this void of mine. Forget about exercising, because I had absolutely zero energy for that. I had no energy for some everyday tasks, not to mention anything extra. I was looking at myself in the mirror, and couldn't recognize myself. It was not me. I lost myself. I was just trying to survive. Every day, trying to get up from the warm, and cozy bed, trying to function as a normal human being, I wondered, "Does anybody else have the hardest time getting out of bed?"

I labeled myself as lazy, I labeled myself as not worthy of a better life. I, myself, was not my biggest cheerleader, so what is there to expect from others? Others wouldn't understand.

A lot of people mistaken occasional bad mood for a depression. It's okay "not to be in a mood" once in a while, but it's not okay to see all bad all the time. There are different types of depression, I'm not a doctor, and I'm not going to go into too much details. There are different versions of depression, there are different triggers for a depression. I would like to think that no one who suffers from depression suffers the same, because all people are unique. There is no one clear answer as to why and how people suffer. Google describes depression as: "low mood or loss of pleasure or interest in activities for long periods of time." But I feel like you can't mistake such a powerful disease once you face it. You will know depression. You will feel it inside.

For me, it was progressively getting worse. At first it started by just being a little quiet. I actually can't even pin point when exactly my depression started blooming. It's silent. It started off just with some low moods, then my low moods became a norm, and it flourished into this incredibly strong storm. A storm that I couldn't handle on my own. I really tried grabbing onto anything and everything that could potentially bring my joy, but nothing was working. I felt like I'm drowning, but I was very much alive. I felt like this huge black hole was sucking me in, slowly but surely, and there was nothing for me to hold on to. I knew I had to take control of the situation, before it was too late, I just didn't know how. Until one day, a miracle happened.

Chapter Two
During

It was a regular day. Nothing out of the ordinary. Weekend. Saturday. Beautiful warm weather outside, May. My husband and I were both home, just chilling, watching TV.

"Oh My God!" I thought to myself.

"Oh My GOD!!!" I screamed as I stormed out of the bathroom. I couldn't contain myself.

I ran up to my husband, and proudly announced, "We are pregnant!"

I was holding a peed-on stick in my hand. Shaking, and crying. My husband hugged me and kissed me. We were so happy. I couldn't believe it. I always knew that my body is like a clock, if you listen closely enough, you can notice everything, my body will tell me. My body is like a clock also because it is always on time, this includes my period. I was just one day late, and no other symptoms were yet present. I thought that maybe these new pills that I'm taking are messing up my cycle. I've decided to take a pregnancy test just because not too long ago we started trying. Only a month ago. From what I see and hear around me, sometimes it's not that easy to get pregnant. Each month you only get about a 20% chance of getting pregnant. Imagine my surprise when I saw those two faint pink lines on the pregnancy test.

After that, nobody knows what to do. You pee on the stick, you see those lines, now what? You pee on another three, six, or eighteen sticks to make sure and to rule out false positives. You then go get a digital test. Then what? All of them tell you that you are with child. I had no idea what comes next. Who do I call? Do I need to go anywhere? Is there a pregnancy line that I'm supposed to inform? Should I start getting ready to give birth? It's funny how we all "kind of" know what's going on, but at the same time, we really have no idea. The feeling of seeing those two lines is unlike any other. Especially when you are trying to get pregnant. When you really, truly want it in your heart. It's astonishing. I think every woman who saw the double line knows what I'm talking about. This feeling comes over you, and it's almost like you can't breathe. At the same time, you are breathing and you are so present in that moment. I couldn't believe it at first. When you see the slow-moving liquid get into the pregnancy test, and you see the first line pop up, which is what is supposed to happen, then you wait for three minutes, you turn the test, and boom…. Your life changed forever.

I called my OB/GYN office right away. It was a Saturday, but the office was open. I told them about my findings:

"I think I have a positive pregnancy test," I told the lady who picked up the phone. I was so unsure of how to proceed, honestly. I was so shocked.

"You 'think' or you got a positive pregnancy test?" she asked.

"Well, I peed on like ten sticks and all of them show up positive." I couldn't contain my happiness, or was it nervousness?

"Okay, let's schedule you for a check-up."

The closest available appointment was in three days. I had to wait. All these days, I woke up in the morning in disbelief that I'm pregnant. I peed on pregnancy sticks every morning, and every time when the second line showed up, my heart skipped a beat. My heart jumped. Butterflies in my stomach. There were birds in my stomach, airplanes, or maybe it was just gas, but either way, it was incredible. Obviously, I was so high up in the sky, my depression was hidden somewhere. It was forgotten. My thoughts flooded with euphoria. The thought of me being pregnant was so surreal. For some reason, it was just shocking and just so unbelievable to me. I always knew I wanted to have kids, but I never actually thought how to have them. I never imagined myself pregnant, I never actually thought about the whole process. I completely skipped this step of pregnancy. For some reason, I thought that kids just appear in your life and you raise them. Also, they appear already grown up. Being like five years old. Of course, I'm joking, but seriously, I never thought about pregnancy. I knew absolutely nothing about kids, so my mind flooded with thoughts of "what if…" From the moment I found out that I'm pregnant, this extreme sense of fear came over me. This fear never left my side.

I understand that everyone is different, and completely unique. It couldn't be more accurate about pregnancy, and I can only speak of my experience. I was a nervous shell of a person. I was reading every day about pregnancy, and fetuses and embryos, and babies. My mind was going into all different directions. One day everything is great, the other, I'm thinking, "What if I miscarry…? What if there is something wrong with the baby? What if I'm going to be a horrible mom?"

I got in my head so much, that I couldn't keep it together some days. It was all dark, then it was all light. I never actually thought about how pregnancy happens. I mean, I know that a man and a woman are supposed to do the "act of love," but what happens after? I was amazed to learn what an incredible path a single sperm has to make in order to get to the egg. I'm not going to go into too much details, but the journey of creating a human is amazing. Your body is going through a lot in order for it to become pregnant. Nothing "just happens." The stars have to align, well, you supposed to ovulate too, but the stars got to be on your side. I came for my appointment very excited, ready to give birth. Little did I know, huh? Pregnancy lasts 40 weeks, on average. The doctor asked me when was the first day of my last period, and from there we found out that I was about 5 weeks pregnant. It was going to be a very long journey.

"But I couldn't be pregnant on my period, I know the date we conceived," I said to the doctor.

"Yes, but that's how your gestational weeks are counted. You have a long way to go."

The nurse came in and took my blood, also I was supposed to pee in a cup. By the way, while pregnant, you will be peeing a lot. After a while urine does not seem as disgusting as you might think. They will have you peeing in cups, in huge jugs, and over all, you will forever want to pee now. From there, my journey began. I made an appointment to come back in three weeks to see if there is a heartbeat.

Those three weeks…. Oh boy. Was I a wreck! Every day I woke up, and I didn't know if I was still pregnant. I was inspecting myself for any signs of miscarriage, every day. I was reading a lot. Knowledge is power, but I wish someone told me to stop it. I immediately stopped smoking, drinking, coffee, sushi, any type of uncured meats, and all the rest of it. I stopped it all. I put myself on hold. I put my life on pause. Reading and watching videos of how the embryo develops and what size is it now? What about now? And now? I wish someone told me that it's a very long road ahead. I wish someone told me that in this state of stress I will be exhausted so much faster. Although, I think, even if someone did tell me that, I would've never listened, because I am my own person. Now, looking back at my pregnancy, I was really nervous throughout the whole process. I think this made my experience even worse.

Waiting for my next appointment those three weeks, I was noticing my symptoms. Now that I knew that I'm pregnant, I was watching myself and my body very closely. I was bloated all the time, I couldn't even suck my stomach in. I was always hungry. When I say hungry, I don't mean just a little hunger, I mean really hungry, like I never ate before. I was hungry to the point when my whole body would start to shake, so I always had a little snack with me. It was caramel candies, something I could chew on. I was told to drink a lot of water, so I was constantly drinking water, even if I wasn't thirsty. I just really tried to make sure my baby had enough of everything. Due to rapidly rising of the hormone that's called progesterone, my sleep was very interrupted. I would wake up in the middle of the night, just wide awake. I couldn't fall back asleep. I was so tired all the time. At first, I thought that it's my anxiety keeping me awake, but after doing my little research, I found out that sleep directly correlates with hormone changes. I wouldn't say that my symptoms were severe, I hear it could've been so much worse. The worst symptom of all, and nobody actually talks about it, was the constipation. I'm not going to go into too much detail, but it was just awful. At one point, I was thinking of calling 911, because of how bad it was, but then I started rationalizing and thinking logically. What will the paramedics do for me in this situation? Give me fluids? I can't take any pills. It was due to the folic acid that I was taking with my prenatal vitamins to help baby grow. Everything is interconnected. All my symptoms were actually considered mild, except for constipation. I had a little nausea, maybe some food aversions, but nothing too serious. The weirdest symptom of all was the restless leg syndrome. It's like my feet were running somewhere, and I couldn't stop it. I couldn't stop it even when I really wanted to. It was the weirdest, harmless, but very annoying pregnancy symptom.

Me and my husband decided not to tell anybody about my pregnancy, because of the uncertainty that the first trimester brings. It was hard. I wanted to share, I wanted the support, but I couldn't. Respecting the agreement between me and my husband, I kept everything to myself. Even though he could never understand what I was going through, and what went on in my mind. He could never experience the things that I was going through on a daily basis. I have decided to keep it to myself, because of the depth of the situation. I knew it's not easy for me, but I also realized that it wasn't easy for him too. Pregnancy and women are usually discussed, but nobody actually talks about how the partners are feeling. The partners take crucial role in our lives, but it's like they're forgotten. I bet there is a lot going on inside your husbands/partners mind while you are pregnant. My husband did not share with me, but I can just imagine the stress because of the unknown.

***

When we came back to the doctor's office in three weeks, nothing was out of the ordinary. I remember asking my husband before the appointment if he wanted to go with me. He was hesitant, because he had to work, but I said: "what if the doctor will say something super important? What if we are having twins?" And we laughed and laughed, but after all, I managed to bring my husband to the appointment with me. We were pretty excited and waited for the doctor to come in the room. When he came in, he introduced himself, because he wasn't my regular doctor and he began the exam. He was an older man, smiling and making little jokes. In the movies they show how a little machine slides on top of your belly, and there you have it, your little baby on the screen. It's not the case in your very early stages of pregnancy. You still have to undress, and you still have to feel all those uncomfortable feelings in the gynecological chair. They look inside your private parts up until you are about 12 weeks of gestation.

The doctor started the exam, and in a minute, he said, "Congratulations, you are having twins!"

Watching as much medical drama as I do, I saw the two sacs on the screen, but I'm not a doctor, what do I know? I couldn't believe it. To say that I was shocked is an understatement. My whole body was trying to process this news. I started crying right there in the chair. Medical assistant was looking at me with such surprise, and a smile. She offered me napkins. Twins do not run in my family, nor my husband's family. How is this possible?

My husband asked, "Is this a joke?"

I was thinking that I'm dreaming, because it cannot be happening. I was in such disbelief. So many thoughts ran through my mind, and yet I cannot pin point a particular one thought. My husband always wanted twins. We were even talking about getting IVF if we ran into trouble conceiving on our own. Well, hubby, no need for that! To both of our surprise, I ovulated two eggs that cycle, at the same time. Our twins are called fraternal. To be exact, dichorionic-diamniotic twins. Which means that each of the babies had its own room, and food supply. I had two placentas, and two amniotic sacs. And just like that, my regular, already exciting pregnancy, turned into a high-risk twin pregnancy. Thankfully it was the lowest risk multiples pregnancy.

Doctor finished the exam and asked us to come in his office. I was still shocked from the discovery. I couldn't stop my tears, maybe it was the hormones, maybe it's just a shocking thing to find out. My knees were barely holding my body. I still couldn't believe that I was pregnant, let alone, I was pregnant with spontaneous twins. My thoughts were racing back and forth, at the same time, I was completely blank. This news was so unexpected, that I think I wasn't even sure how to react to it. I didn't know how I feel about it yet. I needed a minute to breathe.

We came into his office and sat in comfortable red lounge chairs. I was holding my husband's hand and crying. Crying from happiness? The doctor started talking about my pregnancy and how it is automatically a high-risk pregnancy. Even though, it is an optimal twin pregnancy, there are still risks associated with it. There is still a lot that could go wrong. My twins are called dizygotic twins, meaning fraternal, not identical. Doctor explained all the challenges ahead and everything that comes with twin pregnancy. He also explained what I can and cannot do, what I can and cannot eat. He also mentioned that we are at a very early stage and one of the twins can disappear. There were a lot to talk about. He explained that because there are two babies, it will most likely have to be a c-section. Thinking about it logically, what are the chances of both babies being head down when it's time to push? There is simply no room for them to turn, too. The chances are very slim. I was totally okay with having a c-section. The thought of anything coming out of my, excuse me, vagina, was terrifying. He also explained that there are certain risks with trying to deliver naturally. Twin A, which is the baby that is positioned lower in the uterus can come out just fine, but Twin B, who is located higher up in the uterus, could get tangled up in the umbilical cord, and you would still have to have a c-section, but as an emergency, we definitely didn't want to take that chance. It was settled right there and then; I was going to have a scheduled c-section.

Honestly, I wasn't thinking that far ahead. "Let's cross that bridge when we get there," right? I was just told that I'm bringing two human beings into this world, let me just process this information. I wanted to get through this exciting and at the same time scary time, the time where symptoms of life were becoming real, so real. These symptoms of life reminded me that I'm growing two humans inside my body. For a long time, I couldn't wrap my head around this idea, for me, it was so unbelievable. For a long time, I didn't fully realize that I'm pregnant with two babies. My belly really only started to show around 24 weeks. Of course, I understood that I'm pregnant, but for some reason, it was all so magical for me.

To finish up out appointment at the doctor, he informed us that he will not be able to stay my doctor, because twin pregnancies require careful monitoring and it's not his expertise. I should find another doctor. We requested my medical records and left the office. I remember, walking out of the office, me and my husband just paused for a second, hugged, and just laughed. It was just so shocking to find out that we are having twins. I had to find another physician fast, because I was almost at the end of my first trimester. That was another reason for my anxiety, like I didn't have enough. I immediately started calling all the doctor's offices, and asking if they could take me on. All of the doctor's said no, because their schedules are full, or because I was almost at my second trimester, or because I was having twins, or some other reason. I was a nervous wreck. I almost lost all my hope, until one single call:

"Hello?" I could tell by his voice, it was an older man.

"How can I help you?" he asked.

"Hello, I'm looking for an obstetrician, I'm 10 weeks pregnant with fraternal twins," I said with a little hope in my voice.

"Oh Dear! Congratulations! You need a specialist who is specializing in high-risk and multiples pregnancies. I am almost retired. I only work two days out of the week and see only a couple of patients per week. Try calling 'this' hospital."

"I cannot tell you how grateful I am for your advice. Everywhere I called, they just refused to take me on."

"Of course Dear, Good luck with everything!" he said, and hung up the phone.

I finally had a lead. I was happy. I always thought that kindness is free, and some people really remind me of that. I called that hospital that he suggested and they requested my medical records before they could schedule me. I remember thinking that it was the end of the world. I had no doctor, and I thought that I will have to deliver my babies somewhere in a dungeon. My anxiety was not letting me go. After I sent out my medical records to this new facility, they called me back, and asked to schedule an appointment. I found a new doctor! I was so happy. I was so worried about everything, and thinking that that was the biggest problem of all times, but "real" problems came later on. It's all about the perspective, right? At the moment, something might seem so big and so gigantic, and practically unsolvable, but in the big picture of things, I realize that some problems are not even real problems.

We found an office! It was an office in Manhattan, a little far, about 40 minutes from my house, but I didn't care at that point. I didn't really have a choice. They specialized in multiples pregnancies, so that gave me a peace of mind, my babies were in good hands. On our first appointment there, we were very pleasantly surprised, by the staff, and the kindness, and the overall atmosphere. The greeting that we received, and the care that was promised, was all very positive. I felt like a rock-star. The travel time from Brooklyn to Manhattan was well worth it, every single time. I really appreciated the careful monitoring of my babies. Most importantly, I always felt heard. I didn't have to repeat myself twice, every doctor, every nurse, every practitioner knew me by name, as well as my situation and symptoms. This office made my pregnancy feel less scary. All the staff at the reception knew me by name and treated me with utmost respect and excellent service. I am forever grateful for that.

***

Little did I know, that the fear and anxiety will never leave my side now. They were my closest neighbors. It's honestly very exhausting. The funny thing is that nobody really talks about it. Nobody talks about a lot of things in pregnancy, actually. Having said that, I realize that each and every pregnancy is different and completely unique. Everybody has their own symptoms, and fears. The more I read, the more nervous I got, but I couldn't stop reading. I figured, knowledge is wealth, no? I thought that the more information I got, the calmer I will feel during the whole process, but that wasn't the case. Every symptom of pregnancy you get, you of course, google it, and it can go two ways; it's either everything is fine, and it's "normal," or you or your baby is literally dying. It's crazy. One time, I finally read something that made me be okay: "if pregnancy was this easy to mess up, because of an extra cup of coffee, or a cold cut sandwich, we would already be extinct." After this phrase, I kind of let it go, just a little. You can never fully let go, you still worry. I don't know how people did this without internet. Was it better? Or was it worse? How did they know what was normal or not? Actually, in pregnancy, turns out that everything is "normal."

"Doctor, my toe fell off, and my eye is twitching."

"Oh, it's totally normal, that's because you are pregnant."

A lot of anxiety was caused by the hormonal changes in my body. Everybody says that your hormones change during pregnancy, but nobody expands on it. I thought that you just wake up one day and your hormones have changed and adjusted, but no, it happens gradually, throughout your whole pregnancy. Pregnancy hormones are smooth. You don't even notice it that much, it's subtle. Your belly grows slowly. I used to look in the mirror every single day, trying to see my pregnant belly, but patience is key. Pregnancy teaches you patience. You need a lot of it. It kind of prepares you for the baby, because you need a lot of patience with kids as well.

Going through all these changes in your mind and your body, your support system matters. It matters a lot, but you can have the best partner, the best parents, relatives, friends, but you cannot run away from yourself. I mentioned earlier that my coping mechanism with pretty much any situation is running. It's not the case when you are pregnant. You can't run physically, but you also can't run metaphorically. You cannot run away from your thoughts and feelings. It was a very big challenge for me. I felt trapped in my own body and mind. You can have the best partner/ husband, but nobody really knows what you are going through. At the end of the day, you are left alone with your thoughts, with yourself. My husband told me that during my pregnancy I was totally fine, but that's not how I felt. Inside, I was boiling. Pregnancy was definitely a challenge for me. I envy people, women, who go through pregnancy with dignity and grace.

When I was pregnant, I looked very homeless. I stopped wearing makeup, jewelry, and even a pony tail, because I had headaches. I didn't care about my appearance at all. I was very focused on how I'm feeling, which was not the best. I was constantly sweating and couldn't breathe normally. When I was walking, just simply walking, not even fast or anything, I was panting. I was just constantly exhausted. I could barely look at myself in the mirror, because I did not like what I saw there. Everybody kept saying that I'm glowing and I look so good, but I wish I saw that. I wish I wasn't this harsh on myself. Society in general is very harsh on women, we supposed to look a certain way, say certain things, do what we need to do; but I was way too harsh on myself. I didn't really care what society thinks of me, or what I should be doing, but I hated being pregnant. I hated how I feel. It was not magical at all.

Internet was not making it easy on me as well. As much as it helped me, it ruined me too. Everybody on social media was having the best time of their lives being pregnant. Taking pictures, having baby showers, wearing beautiful dresses, gender reveals, traveling, and I thought to myself, "Why I can't be like that? I'm not productive at all. I literally can't do anything."

Watching all these videos with pregnant women "nesting" and cooking the best meals of their lives, here I was, eating my Wendy's burger, tomato is trying to escape my burger, mayo on my shirt, smelling like sweat, and barely breathing. What a time to be alive. I hated myself for being so lazy, not having any motivation, or energy to do anything. But internet helped me too, I can't say it was all bad all the time. Sometimes I came across a video of women who actually struggled through their pregnancies, and they were carrying one child, and honestly, it made me feel better. It made me feel seen, validated, understood. At one point or another you wonder if you're okay, like if you're okay in your mind, and seeing those videos made me realize that I'm still sane. Seeing that I'm not the only one on the planet who is struggling gave me hope and clarity. So I guess I have to thank social media for helping me stay "in my lane." Even though, I could relate to some of the women, I was still hoping and waiting for this magical time to come. The magical time of pregnancy. It never came. Maybe it had to do something with me carrying two babies, but I should've been having twice as much "magic," no?

Let me be completely transparent, I felt blessed from the moment we found out that we were having twins. I am not a big believer in God, but after this, there wasn't a day when I didn't thank him. Every single day, no matter if it was a bad day or a good day, I thanked God. Just in case. I thanked God for letting me be a mother. I thanked God for allowing me to be pregnant each day, because I counted. I counted days, weeks, months. When we got to 24 weeks, which is considered viability, in case something happens and babies had to be born, there is a higher chance of survival. I thanked God. After we got to 32 weeks, which is when the baby's lungs are developed, I thanked God. And every single day after that. I wasn't just thanking God because I needed to, I was thanking him because I felt it inside. I truly, seriously felt in my soul so grateful. During my pregnancy, I recorded my thoughts, I recorded videos of me and my huge, stretched out belly, and that was the best thing I did. Now, watching everything back, I remember. I remember the struggles, I remember how hard it was, I remember the physical and mental load that I carried. I was pushed to the absolute limit, my body, my mind. I thank God for allowing me to experience this to full extend, and for everything I learned during this journey.

As much as I am grateful for my life and my kids, and everything I've been through, I also thank and acknowledge myself. I am an incredible human being, a woman, a mother. I went through so much and I didn't break. I was close, but I didn't break. I have a new found respect for women, for all the mothers. We truly run this world. We are unstoppable. My journey proved to me that I am so much more than just a girl. I am an independent, confident, beautiful person. I have my own thoughts, my own opinions, my own feelings and it matters. My opinions matter. I matter. It's amazing to finally realize it. It's amazing to see how strong I am. It's very refreshing to start getting to know myself for who I truly am. I have a lot of discovering to do, but I will get there. While I was pregnant, I finally was able to put myself first. My self and my babies. I finally was able to say "no." I was able to stand up for myself and it's so important. It's a very important life lesson. I was able to put the family that I'm creating first. I put us on the pedestal and whatever didn't feel beneficial to us, I let it go. I let go of a lot of things.

I guess, what I'm trying to say is that pregnancy changed me. It showed me and opened my eyes to another perspective. I was waiting for this change; I needed this change in my life. I always thought of myself as a teenager, but you grow up so fast. You mature, and you love it. You discover yourself all over again, the new you. It's amazing.

***

When I was about 28 weeks pregnant, I was already huge. I quit my job at the psychiatrist office, because it was very hard for me to move. I was wobbling everywhere. In your second trimester, your bones start to hurt, they loosen up to prepare for birth. I was having horrible pelvic bone pains, my joints were so unstable, at least it felt like it. Every morning I woke up with pain. Pain was everywhere, in my bones, in my fingers, my toes. My feet were so swollen that I had to buy new shoes 2 sizes up. One day, I've decided to go for a walk. I was slowly walking around the block, didn't want to leave the vicinity of my house and I met the sweetest old lady:

"You look beautiful sweetie!" She was walking slowly towards me, pushing her walker in front.

"Thank you. I wish I felt beautiful too," I answered with a big smile on my face.

"Sweetie, you have to wait." She stopped right beside me, and took my hand. "You have to wait until you hold him. When they give you your sweet child, your precious little bundle of joy, you will forget everything."

She was talking so calmly and softly, I could barely hear her. I leaned in forward.

"You have to be patient. God knows what he is doing," she continued. "You just wait."

"You know, I'm actually having twins," I said.

"Oh my God!!! You have been blessed twice!" The excitement in her voice was so genuine. "Just wait, dear. You just wait."

I said, "Thank you for the kind words" and continued walking. She went on her way as well.

"Just wait" comments continued throughout my whole pregnancy. People in the store were coming up to me, commenting on my huge belly: "you are about to pop!" – "I'm having twins, there is still a little bit of time to go." – "just wait." "You just wait." Just wait.... These words will stay with me forever. It seemed like this pregnancy was never going to end, and what am I waiting for? I mean, obviously, my babies, but it was so hard to wait while all the time in pain. I was waiting, there is literally nothing else to do but wait. I didn't understand, I didn't understand why is everybody telling me to wait. Until I knew. Until I found out.

I met a lot of people who were so kind to me. Especially women, mothers, who already went through it. I was surrounded by smiles and kind words. Wherever I went, someone started a conversation with me, sometimes reminiscing their own pregnancy, sometimes words of encouragement, sometimes words of advice. This one time, I met a woman, maybe in her sixties, beautiful, fit woman:

"Sweetheart, are you okay?"

I was sitting on the stairs of some private house, because I walked away too far from home, and just needed a minute to breathe.

"I'm so sorry, I was just taking a break." I immediately started getting up, but getting up with a huge belly is a super task. I was trying to pull myself up, and trying to land on my feet, but I probably looked like a tortoise who accidentally was turned upside down.

"Oh no, sweetheart, have a sit. You rest. You need it." She sat right beside me.

"Thank you, I was just taking my daily walk, and all of a sudden got really tired," I said.

"You know, you are glowing! You look so beautiful."

"Thank you."

"I never got a chance to have children, to be a mother," she started talking. "I always wanted children, but I never had them, it was not in my cards, I guess." She smiled.

"I'm sorry to hear that," I said.

"Oh, that's okay, sweetheart. Let me tell you, when I was about 25 years old, I was pregnant, but very early on in my pregnancy I miscarried. How far along are you, sweetheart?"

"I'm 29 weeks.""

You are almost there! Just a little more to go. After my miscarriage, me and my husband tried again, and again, and then again, but it never happened for us. I guess life is funny like that. We wanted to adopt a child, but my husband was offered an amazing position where we both could travel the world. I didn't have to work and I didn't have to worry about anything. But you know what was the hardest part of it all?" she asked.

"What?"

"To shut my maternal instincts up." She clapped her hands together. "I just closed that door and I refused to be held behind. I went on my merry way into this beautiful world. Childless. Carrying only for myself and my husband. Later we got a dog, but you know, it's not the same…"

"Do you have any regrets?" I asked.

"I think I do. Me and my husband are getting older. We have money, you see, this beautiful house." She pointed at the two story modern house which we were sitting by. "We have great careers, he is an engineer, I am a clothes designer, we've done good for ourselves, but there is no one to share this with. I come home to an empty, quiet house. Soulless house. To be honest, I enjoy it, I enjoy my house, my career, my marriage, but I always wondered what could've been…"

I looked at her face and saw a tear. Just a little, tiny tear sliding down her cheek. She continued, "Sometimes, I dream, I dream that we have 3 or 4 kids, and they all have children of their own, and I'm a granny, just spoiling my grandkids. We all run around this beautiful house, or any other house for that matter. All of this is beautiful, but I can't let myself down, so while it's nice to dream, I can't forget the reality."

She shrugged her shoulders. "Sweetheart, do you want some water?"

"No, thank you, I think it's time for me to go already," I said.

"You are going to be an amazing mother," she said while getting up from the stairs. "Don't let your dreams, ruin your reality, whatever it is."

"It was nice talking to you, thank you for the kind words." As I was walking away, I waved.

"Don't let your dreams, ruin your reality." This phrase stayed with me. I was walking home and thinking. I totally forgot to dream. I was so consumed by this pregnancy, that I simply forgot to dream. I was so preoccupied with everything that's going on, that I haven't allowed myself to paint this beautiful and amazing life of motherhood that I'm about to embark upon. I haven't imagined myself as a mother, I haven't thought about what I want to show my babies. I haven't dreamt at all. My mind was in a constant state of worry, so I haven't allowed myself to dream, I was always so afraid that something will happen to my babies, that I simply forgot to enjoy.

We are constantly running. As a society, we try to be and do everything at once, but where are we running? Everybody knows the end result of life. We are always worrying about money, health, just everyday life, but maybe the key is to stop? Just to stop for a minute and appreciate where you are in life. During my pregnancy I was so concentrated on everything that can go wrong, that I forgot to imagine what if everything goes right? I thought I remained calm and positive, but overall, I was stressed. I was stressed to the point where I forgot to imagine, I forgot to dream, I forgot that it's a once in a life time opportunity, to be pregnant with twins. I always wanted a big family, I always imagined that at 80 years old I will have a table full of people. We are all laughing and smiling, and of course, bickering, but at the end of the day, we are all together. At the head of the table is me and my husband, we started this family, and we are proud. We are proud that we made it.

***

Pregnancy has three trimesters, four if you count postpartum. When I was around 8 weeks pregnant, I wasn't feeling well. Everybody said it's normal, because I'm carrying two babies. One day, something was off. I got to work, and I couldn't leave the bathroom, because I was throwing up. All my body was aching. I had a horrible headache. I called my OB office and they told me to take some Tylenol, it's considered to be safe during pregnancy, but I was hesitant. I stayed at work for about three hours, and called my husband to pick me up. He came and immediately said that he is not feeling well. That's a coincidence, and he is not even pregnant. We came home, drank some hot tea with lemon, took some Vitamin C, but he was getting worse. We decided to take COVID-19 test. His test showed up positive right away, mine showed negative. Talk about double lines all over again, huh? He isolated himself in the bedroom and I stayed in the living room. He had chills, and was sweating, his fever was spiking, we didn't know what to do. I was feeling extremely nauseous and lightheaded.

At night, I started feeling horrible. My fever was 104 °F, I didn't know what to do. I can't take any pills, and I can't really do anything I would normally do. I came to the kitchen, made myself a bowl with iced water, and wet a towel. I laid on the floor and put the towel on my forehead. I put both my hands in the iced bowl. I was so afraid for my babies. The first trimester is very important. The first trimester is when everything is developing. I honestly thought that I was dying. So I did the only thing that was left for me to do, or so I thought; I started praying. I prayed for my kids to be safe and healthy. I prayed to make it to delivery and see my babies. I seriously prayed to stay alive. My fever wasn't breaking, no matter what I did. Around 7 AM we went to the emergency room. When I was waiting, I started crying, because I was so afraid that something could be wrong with the babies. I was no longer afraid for myself, I was afraid for my two miracles. I guess, that's what motherhood is all about.

I was called in and examined. They ran some tests and did another COVID-19 test, which showed up positive this time. An ultrasound tech came in and asked if I wanted to see the babies, to which I of course, answered, yes. He also asked if it's okay if an intern will be present during my exam, because seeing twins on the ultrasound is a rare occasion. I didn't care, I didn't care if the whole hospital would come up to my room, I just needed to know that my sweethearts are okay. He wheeled in the machine, and said that he will try to find them through my belly, if not, then he will do a transvaginal exam. I nodded in agreement. He put the gel on my tummy, and slid the machine on top… there they were, my beautiful peanuts. So tiny, and yet alive and vibrant. He started measuring their heartbeats, everything was looking good. I was finally able to breathe again.

Me and my husband were sick with COVID for about two weeks. It was not fun at all, but also, it was kind of comical, because we got sick in 2022, when COVID was already kind of old news. The first couple of days were brutal, then it was a bit better, but COVID is no joke. I have never in my life felt this shitty. My husband lost his sense of taste and smell, which is like the worst symptom there is. It was a very difficult time for me, because every second of every day I was sick, I was worried about my babies. Thankfully, the fog lifted and we all turned out okay.

***

In your first trimester, you can do prenatal screening. Doctor will draw your blood to check for abnormalities in the fetus. I believe it's optional, if you don't want to know, nobody will make you. In my heart, I felt that everything is going to be okay, I don't know if it's maternal instinct, or just my intuition. I felt calm but worried at the same time. Of course, I wanted this test, I needed to check, I needed to know. The prenatal screening tests for chromosomal abnormalities, there is a lot, but the main three ones are: Trisomy 13, which is Patau syndrome, Trisomy 18, which is Edwards syndrome, and Trisomy 21 - Down syndrome. The results were supposed to come in in about 10 to 14 days, and I was counting. I counted every single day, and checked my email religiously. At the end of day 13, I refreshed my email and saw a subject line that said "test results." My mind went to some dark places. I started imagining all sorts of scenarios. I started thinking, "What if my babies are sick? What if one of them is sick? What are we going to do then?" As much as I wanted to, I didn't click on the email, I didn't open it. I was too nervous. Instead, I called my husband, I asked him if he was home so we can open up the results together.

That was the longest ride home ever. I held my phone in my hand like it was the most important document of my life. I held it like it was the most precious, one of a kind, the most exotic egg and I was afraid to break it. I ran from the train station to my house, opened the door to my apartment and immediately handed my phone to my husband.

With such urgency, I commanded him, "Open it! Open it!"

He opened the email and started reading. He actually started reading from the very top: "Date: June 5th, two thousand, twenty two…. Name…." I was getting so anxious. I couldn't wait for him to stop playing around.

"Negative. Negative. Negative." He finally got to the part with important information.

I grabbed my phone from his hand and started reading myself. I had to see it for myself. Everything was negative. "No abnormalities detected." It was like a mountain was lifted off of me. From the nervousness and chaos that I've created in my head, myself, I was so tired, I started crying to release some of the tension. We then continued to look through the results…

"Look! Predicted twin fetal sexes: Male/Male! We are having two boys! Two sons!" my husband shouted with such excitement.

And that was our gender reveal party…. Just the two of us, standing in our kitchen, crying and sweating from the summer heat, well, and my pregnancy hormones.

That day we found out that not only our babies are perfectly healthy, but also that they are two boys. How exciting! I always wanted my first born to be a boy, but when I actually got pregnant, it didn't matter. I honestly didn't care if it's going to be two boys, two girls, boy and a girl, I only cared that they are safe, happy and healthy. I now understand when people say that they don't care who they are having, or better yet, waiting until birth to find out. It truly doesn't matter. You will love this little child with all you have, and you will dedicate your whole self to this child, whatever the gender.

We weren't completely out of the woods yet, this screening only tests for any genetic disorders and chromosomal abnormalities. We also had to find out if the babies were physically developing normally. That ultrasound is done right around the middle of your gestation, around 20 weeks. At 20 weeks we went for our anatomy scan. That's where they look at all the organs, brains, hands, feet, toes and fingers and all the rest of it. We came early, as usual, because even pregnant I was freakishly uptight about our timing for our appointments. We were waiting in the waiting room, and I was listening to myself. I learned to listen to myself, but most importantly, I learned to trust myself. I learned to trust my feelings. This time, my gut was once again, keeping me calm. I asked myself, "Is everything going to be okay?" And in my mind, I answered, "Yes."

We were called into the room and the scan started. Because it's twins, the whole appointment took about 40 minutes. We counted the fingers, and the toes, we saw the big round bellies of my sweethearts and as I thought, everything looked good. One of the babies even showed us a thumbs up. That was pretty funny.

Being pregnant really showed me a different perspective. I saw how strong I am. Physically, of course, because my boys were weighing each like a singleton baby, a baby who is in the womb alone. By the end of my pregnancy, Twin A was around 6 pounds, and Twin B was at around 7 pounds. Plus two placentas, and two amnionic sacs, I was carrying around 20 pounds just in my belly alone. Turning in bed was such a struggle, it was like a bag of bricks just holding me down. Getting up from the bed was the worst, and when you have to pee like a million times per day, it really takes a toll on you. Besides the physical aspects, seeing how strong I am mentally, really gave me strength to push forward. It gave me hope and belief that I can do anything. I was chosen for this because I can actually do it. Every week I was pregnant I counted, and celebrated. Each week felt like such an accomplishment. And it really was. Twin pregnancies, and in general, multiples pregnancies, are unpredictable. Babies could simply run out of room to grow, and then water can break early, high blood pressure is a possibility, it's actually called preeclampsia - another fancy word I learned. I was doing good. I carefully monitored every move they make, and oh boy, they were making moves. Towards the end of my pregnancy, their kicks and little jabs were not pleasant at all, it was very painful. I stopped driving at around 25-26 weeks because I was afraid to lose control of the wheel, because of how hard my babies were punching me. When they were awake at the same time, I could literally see one leg on one side of my stomach, and the other leg on the other side of my stomach, it was a scary scene. It was also incredible, but very painful.

***

Overall, the "magical" kicks that everyone is talking about, weren't as magical, as I imagined. I started feeling my babies kick at around 17-18 weeks. One evening, I couldn't find a comfortable spot in the bed and I felt really nauseous. I thought something bad was going to happen, because my heart started racing. I was lying in bed and breathing, trying to keep myself calm. After a while, I felt a little kick. I couldn't believe it. Doctors say that you supposed to start feeling the kicks around 18-24 weeks, but I was right at that spot. I didn't think it was going to happen so soon for me. At first, it was just like little waves in my stomach, just a slight tiny touch, and every time I felt lightheaded, almost like my organs were moving inside of me. Such an odd feeling. After that, in about a week or so, I really started to feel their kicks. Their legs became stronger as they grown inside of me and those kicks become more and more visible. That's when I calmed down a little. When you can feel your baby move, it means that they are okay and alive. Since I had two babies, I kind of knew where each of them was lying, so I could differentiate who was kicking. That's when you're supposed to start counting the kicks. I believe it was supposed to be 10 kicks in a 24 hour period.

My babies were pretty active, so I really didn't have to worry about counting kicks, until one day. I was still at work, and all of a sudden I felt like something was off. I was just sitting in a chair, doing my job and I thought to myself, "I haven't felt Twin B today." Usually, during the day, babies are sleeping, because you kind of rock them to sleep while walking. They wake up at night, when you are peacefully lying in bed or sleeping. But I felt something was off. I nervously started remembering when was the last time I felt him kick, but because I was already in a panic mode, I couldn't. I called my husband worrying. He said that it's probably nothing, that he is probably just sleeping and I am worrying for no reason. But I couldn't shake this feeling. I ate lunch, I drank some sweet juice to wake him up, but nothing was working. I only felt Twin A. I officially started to get worried.

I asked to get off work early, and went straight to the emergency room. Thankfully, it wasn't far from my job, so I walked there, in hopes that I will wake Twin B up. I got to the emergency room and checked in, they asked, "What brings you in?"

"I'm pregnant with twins, and I think I haven't felt one of the babies kick today," I said with such worry in my voice.

"Okay, darling, have a seat," the receptionist said.

I sat in a chair and started shaking my leg, like I usually do. I was getting really nervous. In the emergency department, they sort out the patients by urgency of their situation. If you come in with blood all over the place, you will be seen right away, chest tightness will also get you in pretty quick, pregnancy with twins with a possibility of no fetal movement is a first in line type of situation. A nurse came down from the labor and delivery department, and called my name. I had to sit in a wheelchair, and she was taking me up to see the doctor. The nurse tried to make small talk with me, but I just couldn't, I was consumed by my worry about my child. I was pale and could barely hold myself. I briefly explained what's going on, and kept quiet. She told me not to worry and that it happens sometimes, but until I see the two heartbeats on the monitor, I wasn't going to relax. We got to the labor and delivery floor, and I was immediately greeted with warm smiles and kind words.

"I hear twins are in the building! How did you get so lucky?" One of the nurses came up to me and started getting me situated in the triage.

"I honestly don't know, these are spontaneous twins, they don't run in our families." I smiled.

"Okay, sweetheart, let's hook you up to the machine. Do you mind if I call some interns to ask you questions? Besides, everybody would love to see twins! Twins are not as common as you might think," she asked.

"I don't mind," I said.

Four girls came in in white coats with little notepads. They took turns asking questions. I could tell they were fascinated by my twin pregnancy, but also medicine in general. They were asking me what kind of symptoms I have, and how did I react when I found out that I'm carrying twins. They took my mind off my worry for a second. The doctor came in and started the exam. He turned the monitor towards me:

"I see two heartbeats," he said. "Now, let's try and listen." He turned up the volume.

Tic-a-tic-a-tic-a-tic. I heard loud and clear.

"Now, let's listen to Twin B."

Tic-a-tic-a-tic-a-tic-a-tic.

I sighed with such relief. I had tears in my eyes, because of the exhaustion from all the worrying.

"Why are you crying? They are okay. Everything is okay," the doctor said.

"I don't know, I didn't know what to think, I was worried sick," I said.

"No need to worry, they are just sleeping."

The doctor started showing the interns where and how Twin A was lying, and where was Twin B. Where the placentas were, and all the rest of it. I felt like a rock-star. The interns were taking notes, and I was instantly in a better mood. I was ready to talk about my babies all day long.

In the evening, when I got home, I told my husband that I went to the emergency room, because I was worried, he sat in front of my belly and said, "Guys! You can't make mom worry! It's a long road ahead, you have got to be on your best behavior! You hear me guys?"

He kissed my belly two times, one kiss for each baby. That melted my heart.

"It's never going to be just the two of us anymore. We will constantly be running around with kids and our dog, I'm afraid that we will lose each other," I told him and put on a song, "Just the two of us" by Grover Washington Jr and Bill Withers.

"Don't worry, we will always find our way back to each other," my husband replied.

Later that week, he asked me on a date. I had no idea where we going, but I knew that it had to involve food. I got dressed and even put make up on. Of course, before we left, I had to use the restroom. I slowly wobbled to the bathroom and sat on the toilet.

I looked down and saw spots of blood on my underwear. My mind is apparently not my best friend, because the thoughts that popped up in my head couldn't be any darker. I came out of the bathroom and told my husband.

"What do you want to do?" he asked.

I was so exhausted from not sleeping and all the worrying that I've been going through. I once again asked myself, "Is everything okay?" And the answer was once again, "Yes." I was so excited to go on this date. I was ready for our date. After talking it out, we've decided to go to our date, and after that go to the emergency room. After all, I had to eat, anyway. I tried to let it go and enjoy "just the two of us." I had no pain, no cramping, no gushing of blood, no unusual symptoms, just a little spotting. It was in the back of my mind, but I trusted myself.

We were headed to the airport. Oh, the suspense! Imagine we were flying somewhere? Not in the third trimester! Actually, with me, not in any trimester, I'm too paranoid. I wouldn't be able to enjoy a vacation. Turned out we were headed to the closed terminal, that used to be a real terminal, but it was turned into a hotel and a restaurant. The waitress seeing my huge belly greeted us with a big smile and sat us at a table. We had a small chat, and ordered food. We had a great time. Me and my husband enjoyed ourselves and it was the last time we were alone. Looking back, I actually appreciated this date even more. We finished our meal, which was delicious by the way, and it was time for us to go. We were headed to the emergency room.

At the hospital, I was once again hooked up to the baby monitors. The doctor found two heartbeats, and everything looked good. I was told that spotting happens sometimes, because pregnancies are unpredictable. It was yet another stressful situation but we handled it very well. The best part of it was that not one time I felt like I was out of place. Each time when I came into an emergency room with a concern, I was always carefully examined and doctor and nurses never made me feel like I'm "too much" or like I'm imagining things, or like I'm being too paranoid. The opposite, I was always told that if there is anything at all that bothers me, I should always come in. I was told: "If you feel something is happening or you are concerned about anything at all, you should always come in and get checked out."

***

Pregnancy took a toll on me, physically of course, but mentally... oh my god. The mental load while you are pregnant is crazy. I was terrified. One of my biggest fears was stillbirth. It's when the baby is born sleeping, meaning not alive. I was terrified by this thought. It happens unexpectedly and nobody can predict it. Nobody can warn you about it, there are no indications. It just happens. Probably very selfish of me, but I thought, "I'm going through so much pain, and God forbid, stillbirth?!" It was only later on when I realized, that it's not about the pain during pregnancy, it's not about what you are going through that will make heart shatter, it's not about you at all actually. It's all about the baby.

My intrusive thoughts were not letting me go. I had this horrible vision about one of my twins being born sleeping, and I couldn't breathe. I couldn't shake it. This thought was living in my mind rent free and I was absolutely numb and helpless. Once again, nobody in my circle of friends or acquaintances had anything like that happen, but for some reason, once I learned that it can happen, I was just not myself. This fear stayed with me up until I had my babies. For 37 weeks, I carried my babies and this stupid thought. For 37 weeks I was not able to let it go. For 37 fucking weeks.

This thought alone was exhausting me and brought so many dark, unimaginable feelings and images. This thought nearly destroyed me. After the babies were born, this stupid thought went out the window so fast. I never thought about it ever again, but this experience showed me that I probably won't be getting pregnant ever again. I just couldn't imagine myself going through everything again. I wonder if second time around it would've been different. I guess will never know. I can't risk it.

Maybe it was my depression in disguise making me "crazy." I just wasn't able to "label" it as depression because I was preoccupied being pregnant with twins. My mind was playing tricks on me. My depression was my roommate? I don't know. I know I was depressed on some level, but I had a lot going on, I was too busy googling my symptoms. The funniest thing is that I don't think there is anything that anybody could've told me that would make me feel better. And I guess, nobody could've differentiated my depression from my pregnancy, because symptoms are very similar. While pregnant, you are tired all the time; while depressed, you are also very tired and have no energy for anything. Intrusive thoughts, dark images, imagination running wild, all part of pregnancy, but also depression. During my pregnancy I was talking to my therapist, and I was taking care of myself in that sense, because I was all alone. I was all alone with my thoughts and my stupid dark images. My therapist was trying to make it better for me, but I am my own person, I was thinking what I was thinking and there was nothing anybody could've done.

Sometimes I wonder, if I wasn't suffering from depression, would my pregnancy be a better experience? I honestly don't know. I wish I could roll back the tape and just relax, but it's very hard. Pregnancy is a very traumatic experience. It's a life-altering, traumatic experience for any woman, not just someone who suffers from depression. Growing a human being inside of you, let alone two, is very challenging, and it takes everything from you, in every aspect.

***

In your first and second trimesters, you see your doctor every four weeks, which is, trust me, a very long time to wait. The whole pregnancy is pretty much a waiting game. Starting at approximately 28-29 weeks, you start seeing your doctor every two weeks, which is where things get a little more fun. At around 34-35 weeks you start going to the doctor every single week, that was the best. I got to see my babies and talk delivery plan. My delivery plan or birthing plan was pretty simple, to survive. I didn't have any special instructions, just to survive. As you can see, my wishes were answered.

I decided pretty early on that I was going to have a c-section. As expected, one of the twins was breach, which means butt down. It was finally time to schedule my c-section. I did my little research, which date should we pick, how the stars align, what is the most favorable date to deliver a child. I was reading all kinds of "old wives' tales" and finally made my decision. We were going to have our babies on January 10th. Honestly, we were planning to have a January baby, a Capricorn baby, but if it was a singleton pregnancy, the due date was actually falling on the end of January and beginning of February. But, because it was a multiples pregnancy, they rarely go to term, and our "predicted" due date was January 17th.

January 10th was marked on my calendar; we were all good to go. Hospital was advised, and ready for us, but most importantly we were ready. We didn't know what we are ready for, but we were ready. I was so excited to be done with pregnancy. I was so excited to not feel the constant pain anymore. I was so ready to become a mom. It is only a matter of time when I learned that you can never be ready for it. You can actually never be ready to become a mom. Days were passing by, nights were passing by, I was excited in anticipation for the birth of my little beans. On January 5th I received an email with instructions. I had to get my blood drawn, and get a COVID test, so did my husband, because he was going to be in the delivery room with me. We went and got everything done on January 6th. My surgery was scheduled for 8 AM, so the arrival time at the hospital was supposed to be 6 AM. I was already living and seeing that day….

But… you can plan all you want, once again, pregnancy is unpredictable. By the end of my pregnancy my husband was already sleeping on the couch, because I never could get comfortable in our king sized bed. I was huge and in a lot of pain. I was making all kinds of noises while turning in bed, plus the constant urge to go to the bathroom. It was beneficial for us to sleep in separate rooms. One day, I couldn't fall asleep and was watching something on Hulu, as I always did. I was watching series on my phone until about 1 AM. I finally found a position that I was somewhat comfortable in, and drifted off to sleep. At exactly 2 AM, I woke up to go to the bathroom, but something was happening. It took me a minute to get up from my bed, but when I did, I felt warm water was running down my legs. Two days before my scheduled c-section, my water broke. I was 37 weeks and 1 day pregnant. I couldn't believe it. The realization of what just happened settles in and you have to act. My water was leaking everywhere. I wobbled to the living room and in complete darkness whispered, "Babe, I think my water broke."

My husband did not flinch. He showed zero signs of distress. While I was a wreck. He said, "Don't worry, the babies are coming! We were preparing for this!"

I was standing in the living room, leaking amnionic fluid all over the place. I was shaking. I was preparing for this for nine months, but you can never be ready. I knew that delivery day was coming, but it was somewhere in the future, not right now. But it was now, it was happening right now.

My husband grabbed the hospital bag that I had prepared since my 32nd week. He brought a bunch of clothes for me to wear. I was just so out of my element. I think it was the first time when I actually, seriously panicked. I was calling my OB office for the instructions, even though, at this point the instructions are pretty clear: your water breaks, you go to the hospital. At one point, I thought to myself that I should be brave and I should shield my husband from my emotions and mask it. I didn't. I am so glad I didn't. I was just reacting to a situation. How can you not freak out when you about to become a mom to two kids? This is the biggest responsibility of my life. This is the hardest thing I have ever done, meaning pregnancy, and motherhood in the nearest future. I have already pushed my body to the limits and was about to push my mind and my mental state beyond. Standing in my living room, with my legs spread out wide, wet and uncomfortable, I realized that there was no other person on this planet that I would rather be with right now than my husband. He got dressed and helped me get dressed. He told me to wait while he gets the car. Everything is a blur after that, to be honest, even though I think I remember that night like it was yesterday, I don't think I will ever forget it. We put pee pads in the car, because there was a lot of water coming out of me. He helped me get in the car and off we went. We were going to the most important meeting of our lives. We were going to meet our children.

It was a relatively short ride to Manhattan, no traffic, no people, 2 AM. Sunday night. On the way there, I recorded a video, with happy tears in my eyes, listening to Mr. Drake on the radio, we were headed to change our lives forever. During pregnancy, I learned how important it is to record everything, because you forget. You forget a lot of things. Pregnancy is a traumatic experience, it's a life-altering traumatic experience, but our mind plays a trick on us and we tend to forget. Now, I look back at my videos and smile, or cry. It's a spectrum of emotions. I feel such pride. Women's bodies are amazing. Just incredible. We are so strong. We are unstoppable. We put ourselves through so much and we bravely go through it, all alone. By ourselves. The amount of respect I have for women is endless. We got to the hospital and I had to go in alone while my husband looked for parking. I came in and asked the receptionist where do I go, she showed me to the elevator and called the labor and delivery floor to meet me. I was so nervous, but at the same time, I was so excited. So excited to meet my sweethearts. My pregnancy was finally done, I am at the final destination. I was examined to make sure that it was my water that broke and I didn't just pee my pants. Everything checked out.

I have to say something about the nurses. Nurses are literal angels on earth. The amount of attention I got, the help, the reassurance, and kind words. I have no words to explain how grateful I am for the staff that helped me. One nurse took my hand and showed me where I can change into a gown. She saw my watering eyes and held my hand a little longer.

"Look at me," she said very firmly.

"Look at me, sweetie. You are going to be just fine. Your babies are coming. Pull yourself together and get ready to meet them," she said.

I couldn't say a word. I nodded. I felt faint. My palms were sweaty and I couldn't breathe properly. I got changed and she helped me get on the bed. I was hooked onto the machines one last time. Doctor came in and examined me. One baby was still breach, but she still asked me if I wanted to try pushing, to which I answered no, because it was going to be a c-section anyway. My husband came shortly after and we were on our way to meet our sweet peanuts. I was wheeled into a room where I had my IV hooked up. Oh, the pain! But comparing to the pregnancy pains, this was a walk in a park. After all the preparations were done, I was asked to walk into an operating room.

It was officially happening. I couldn't believe it. It was like yesterday that we found out we were having twins, and now, we are actually having them. My nerves were like guitar strings, stretched to the limit. I didn't want my husband to leave my side, I was holding his hand so tight. I had to go and get prepped for the surgery. C-section is considered to be a major surgery. In order to get the baby, a surgeon has to go through seven layers of body. First, there is the skin, then subcutaneous fat, fascia, muscles, peritoneum, uterus and finally the amnionic sac. For those who think that a c-section is an easy way out, you couldn't be more wrong. It's a real surgery, with a possibility of complications and extensive recovery. I sat on a surgical table and was prepped. I got my epidural and anesthesia and was laid and strapped to the table. My c-section was also a way of me to try and control at least something during this hard time, but I couldn't get a hold of my emotions. There were a lot of people in the room, everybody was there for me and my babies. Everybody was ready. The nurses were trying to calm me down and talk to me. The doctor came in and introduced himself. Everything was happening so fast. I was constantly telling them I can't move my legs, to which they reassured me that this is exactly what is supposed to be happening right now because the epidural is working. A huge, blue sheet of material rose in front of my face. I was all ready for the surgery. "Interesting" conversation was going on between me and the anesthesiologist. I was so nervous, I was constantly asking him if I was okay, he always answered yes. I asked him: "I'm so nervous, can you please talk to me?" To which he said: "about what?" I understand that it was a very early morning, and not everybody's lives are changing at this very minute, but come on dude! I asked him: "do you have any children?" He said "yes, two" His answer just cut me off, it was so dry and so unpleasant. I was really hoping that my hubby is coming soon.

    The nurses finally called my husband in, he was wearing a hospital gown, a hat and shoe covers. He sat right next to me as the doctor was getting ready for the delivery. I couldn't stop talking, I guess, from the nervousness. I kept asking the anesthesiologist if I was okay. To which the answer was always yes, I was totally fine.

    The doctor started talking, "Making an incision."

I held my breath. I was so afraid to move and mess up the surgery. I kept on saying, "I think I'm falling off the table, I can't move my legs."

Nurses once again reassured me that I'm very secure on the table, and everything is okay. Meanwhile, my husband was holding my hand and I continued, "Are you recording? Record everything! I'm not going to remember this! Record everything!"

He, in fact, did not record anything. Honestly, I understand that, he wanted to be in the moment. He wanted to capture everything in his mind. But I wanted it in our memories forever.

"Making an incision in the uterus."

And in a moment we heard a strong, but tiny voice... the cry of my firstborn child.

"Twin A is out. Time of birth 6:20 AM."

I could feel this warmth, this incredible sense of happiness in my heart. And the relief... the relief that I felt was so freeing. I could finally breathe again.

"Twin B is out."

But there was no crying.

"Is he okay? Is my baby okay???" I immediately started panicking. "Tell me, is he okay?"

"Time of birth 6:21 AM. He is perfectly fine, we are just cleaning him up," one of the nurses said.

"Why isn't he crying? Is he okay?" I asked again.

"He swallowed some amnionic fluid, he is just fine...."

There it was.... My second born started crying. Just a little bit. Just for a couple of seconds, but he was alive. That's all that mattered. My baby B started breathing. My sweet baby B was crying. I was free. I felt like a bird that just learned to fly. I felt like I have achieved the ultimate freedom.

It was done. In just two minutes I became a mother to two beautiful baby boys. Actually, I think I became a mother from the moment I found out I was pregnant. The birth just solidified my feelings.

Chapter Three
After

I was so happy that my pregnancy was done. I have gone through the most challenging and hardest thing ever. Or so I thought. Time flew by, it's true, but I don't miss it one bit. I still look at myself in the shower and try to wrap my head around of what happened. The stretch marks, lose skin, discoloration of the skin, all the extra weight on my hips, thighs and stomach, the postpartum hair loss and the stink that my body produces now, the random hairs that come up out of nowhere on my stomach, weird sensations inside of me and my scar... Who am I? After the birth of my children I couldn't look at myself in the mirror, because I didn't recognize who was staring back at me. I didn't recognize myself. It wasn't me. I used to be afraid of my scar. Time healed it. Time healed me. Now, I'm proud of my scar. I birthed two beautiful humans. I did that. My body did that.

After the surgery, under all the drugs, I kept telling the nurses that I can't walk. They smiled at me and gently tapping on my shoulder said, "No need to walk sweetie." That feeling of completely not being able to feel my legs is actually very scary. I thought to myself: "oh my God, this is what a paralyzed person is going through" And this thought brought another dimension to this situation. I was worried that I might never get to feel my legs again and that was terrifying.

I remember being wheeled out of the operating room and I saw the doctor who performed my c-section and I was so grateful. My heart was full. I couldn't even express how grateful I was. I kept on saying thank you, thank you so much… I really meant it. Thank you so much.

And so it began, my fourth trimester, my motherhood journey. Having kids does change you. You become a different version of yourself. A better one. Now, I was responsible not only for myself, but for two cutie pies, who completely depended on me. Kids do bring you joy, they really do, and the love is there, right away, at least that's what happened to me. I felt enormous love for my children. Or maybe it was the drugs. Kids teach you patience. They teach you that nothing is forever. They also show you the person you married or had these children with. It's important to choose wisely. When those 3 AM feedings hit, and both of you hadn't had a decent amount of sleep in a while, trust me, it builds up. The father of your children is so important. I saw my husband in a different light. I always knew he was going to be a great dad, but it's not that simple. Doing the bare minimum will never be enough. It's not only about the diapers and the feedings. It's actually about your communication as two adults. My husband made me fall in love with him all over again. When my husband became a father, his inner man, his confidence, his growth mentally, showed up so unexpectedly. It is so satisfying watching him with his kids. It is so incredibly beautiful overseeing his curiosity about his children and me, his wife. There wasn't a day where he didn't say "thank you for all you do" to me. There wasn't a day when I didn't feel seen. It is so important, it is so valuable, to be seen. I really think that if it wasn't for him, I might of never made it.

My husband, standing 6 feet tall, handsome, green-eyed, blonde man, showed me another perspective on life. A perspective so different from my parents and the society I lived in. We have been through a lot, ups and downs, good and bad, but the good overweighs by so much. During the second part of my pregnancy, when babies started kicking, and my belly was the size of a melon, I started grieving our relationship. I knew that everything had to change. Our next chapter was called "just the four of us and the dog." The full house. Just like I always wanted. I am so happy about it, don't get me wrong, I feel truly blessed, but there is a part of me that misses "us." That's another thing that nobody talks about. Your life completely changes once you have kids and you have to adjust. The baby doesn't have to adjust, the baby doesn't know what's going on, but you do. You start missing the little parts of your life that you took for granted.

After you have kids, your life changes, you change, your partner changes, your relationship changes. You both now have to maneuver through the challenges and the way you do it is major. At the newborn stage, you both are in survival mode. I would say the first year is pure chaos. All of you just trying to stay alive. So yea, your communication as two adults better be on point. I saw a video one time, where a woman said, "In the very first year of having a baby, don't talk about divorce, don't even mention it." We lived by it. It's not because love disappears, or something happens between the two of you, it's because you are in pure survival mode. In survival mode there is no sugar coating, there is no "being careful with your words," there are only raw emotions. Emotions are running high. You don't always have the patience. You are constantly thinking of your baby and just staying alive. Honestly, it's brutal.

You go into this zone of roommates for a while. A lot of people, including us, do shifts with newborns. Because newborns eat around the clock. Even at night. What? My husband was more functional at night, so I only saw him for a couple of minutes before I went to bed. We exchange a couple of words about the babies and off to bed I went. I honestly thought that the hardest part of parenting was going to be raising decent human beings, but the newborn stage completely kicked our butts. Your energy runs out fast.

Before we found our routine, we slept on average 2-3 hours per day and you really can't function on such little sleep. Having one baby is easier, having two babies and absolutely no help is chaos. For a while you forget about each other. For a while, you become partners, partners in a business that you have no idea how to run. Partners with one goal in mind: to survive and keep your little precious cargo alive. Sometimes you bicker, sometimes you fight, but it's important to find your way back to each other.

***

It was a rocky road. The newborn stage... oh boy! The first 3-4 months, you are taking care of a potato. There is absolutely no communication between you and the baby. I, personally, haven't even held a baby this tiny in my life, and here I was, trying to take care of two at the same time. I seriously have PTSD from the newborn stage. It was so hard for me. Sometimes I get flashbacks, sometimes I remember those nights, I get goosebumps remembering everything we've been through.

My thoughts flooded with worry and questions about my kids. These two human beings, tiny people have taken over the world. My world. I guess, it's normal? It's normal for a mother to become this obsessed with her kids, but I missed me. Not the old me, not the new me, just me as a person. Who am I? I have yet to find out. My energy has officially finished, but my life hasn't even begun. When will I get back to "normal"? Actually, I don't need normal, I need extra. I have tried a lot of remedies, but nothing gets me this boost of energy that I need. When it's 9 AM, and you've been up since 4 AM, and you washed all the bottles, and you changed 6 diapers, no wonder I don't have the energy, it's practically midday. I'm simply tired. That would've been no problem, if my kids didn't need my energy, to survive. I have to give, but there is nothing left. They need me all day, every single day.

The newborn stage completely destroyed me. Before becoming a mom, I didn't even think about how important food is for a baby. You just don't think about it. Just like I never thought about how many times per day I eat, maybe twice? A baby eats around the clock, every two - three hours. I had no idea, I honestly never thought about it. Some people will say that the newborn stage is the easiest one, because all baby is doing is sleep and eat. I completely disagree. The newborn stage crushed me. At one point, I didn't think we were going to make it. Because of sleep deprivation, and everything that's going on, you forget to take care of yourself. And that's crucial.

At the hospital, I had a lactation specialist come in and show me how to feed my boys. It was brutal. She shoved my boob in my angel's mouth, I couldn't even see his face. I was so surprised. It wasn't at all like they show in the movies, where a mother gently rocks her baby and offers him her breast, and he starts to eat and everybody is so happy. Blah, blah, blah. For us, it was such a task. A task that we did not succeed in. My sweethearts did not latch. So now what? I'm not going to have this connection with them? This closeness? This incredible mother-son unity? I was so upset. At the same time, I was kind of relived. I thought my milk is not going to come in. Turns out, milk comes in after a couple of days of delivery. I thought that I will just feed them formula, which I had no problem with. On the second day at the hospital, I was introduced to a pumping machine. I did not yet realize that it was going to become my nightmare.

When you start producing milk, the first thing that comes out is called colostrum. It's orange-ish, kind of thick substance, full of nutrients and health benefits.

It's important for a baby to drink it, because it gives them immune system and helps fight infections and stuff like that. Then in a couple of days your actual milk comes in. You can actually feel it in your breast. They become full, and enlarged. In the hospital, I was provided with a pumping machine that was connected by a wire to an outlet. I knew I wasn't going to be able to be tied down to a chair at home, so I ordered a portable pumping machine. It was a game changer. Until I realized that I'm never taking those soul-sucking machines off of me. We put our babies on a strict schedule, a lot of people also disagree with that, because "you're supposed to follow your babies' lead."

Not when you have multiples. All rules go out the window when you have multiples. We were feeding them every three hours. In order to feed them every three hours, I had to produce milk, and pump. A pumping session is usually 20-30 minutes, and because I had two babies, I always did 30 minutes. So I was pumping every two hours. Every two hours! Every two hours machines were sucking on my nipples until they bled. First couple of days it was not that bad, but then... Then it became a burden. Every time I put those things on me, I felt like my life was literally being sucked out of me. I felt like I was dying. Every time I had to pump, I had this unshakable feeling of dread. I had tears in my eyes. Very often I cried while pumping. I cried because of the emotional toll, but also the physical.

After about two weeks of pumping, my nipples started cracking. It was very painful. Not too long after that, they started bleeding. No matter how much cream and lotion I put on, nothing was helping. No matter what I did, I was in so much pain. Again. Pain. It was only at my postpartum appointment at my OB office, where I found out that I have something called dysphoric milk ejection reflex. For a while there, I thought I was crazy. I was watching videos of women pumping and enjoying it? I shrug my shoulders and scrolled, because of how miserable I was. It wasn't me. I wasn't the mom who enjoyed it either. I was once again, thinking that there was something wrong with me. I even tried "adjusting" my attitude towards pumping, and I really tried not to hate it that much, but I couldn't. With a huge smile on my face, I cried. I cried and cried again. People breastfed their children until they go to college, and here I was, couldn't even make it to one year. Of course, I'm joking, but there was nothing funny about it at that point. I had so much resentment towards myself.

"What kind of mother I am, my only job is to feed my babies, and I can't even do that?" My thoughts were destroying me. I was not headed in the right direction at all. I felt so much guilt all the time, but I will expand on it a little later.

The guilt around your milk supply is real. I was pumping for twins. I was pumping nonstop. Your milk supply is based on demand, so technically, the more you pump, the more milk you will produce. By the end of my pumping journey, which lasted two months, I was producing 80 ounces of milk per day. It's about 2,500 liters of breastmilk. Every ounce is 30 milliliters and it uses 20 calories of your body's energy to produce it. So, if I'm doing my math correctly, I had to eat around 2,500 calories just for the milk, and then on top of that another minimum of 1,500 calories to sustain myself. Long story short, I was hungry all the time, and I was malnourished. I did not eat nearly enough, because I had no time. Considering that one baby is demanding, imagine having two at the same time. I had no time to go to the bathroom, not to mention eating. I was not taking good care of myself. Hell, I did not take care of myself at all. Besides, you supposed to prepare the food, but I had no energy to do so and you can only order out so much. I could eat an entire pizza pie by myself and still felt hunger. I dropped almost all my 70 pounds that I gained during pregnancy during these two months of pumping. I was a shell of a person. Sleep deprived, hungry, bleeding nipples and a lot of crying. Almost like a zombie, minus the crying. It was not at all how I imagined motherhood to be. It was so far from that "perfect picture" in my head.

Having said that and having what I went through, I realize how proud I am. I am so proud of myself. I'm proud of the sacrifices that I have made, because I was able to make them, because I wanted to make them. I became a mother to two beautiful boys and I am so incredibly proud. I try to realize every single thing that I have achieved already in this time that I have been a mom. I am proud of all the women. We are so strong, and I'm not going to get tired of repeating myself. We are so strong for ourselves, for our kids, for our partners. Women are superior. I want to cry because of all the sacrifices that I've made, but cry from happiness, because I was able to make them. I put myself second, or even third all the time, because I am able to and I'm okay with that. I am so grateful for my kids and I thank God every single day for allowing me to be their mother. I learn from them just as much as they learn from me. I have sacrificed my body, my mental health, my physical health, but as time goes by, I realize that it wasn't for them, it was for me. I needed my babies more than they needed me. I needed to feel what I feel. I needed to feel this incredible love, I needed to feel all these feelings and emotions that motherhood brings. I was given one body for this life time, and I did the absolute best thing with it. There is not a dime of regret. The extra weight, the soggy boobs after breastfeeding, the stretch marks, the c-section scar, this is all mine, and I'm proud.

***

Oh…the guilt. The guilt stayed with me for a while. For a very long while. I don't think it's gone yet. The guilt that I felt was eating me alive. I felt guilty for everything I did and didn't do. I never thought that this feeling of guilt can be so strong. This constant guilt that I was feeling took away the little energy I had left. I was exhausted. I was feeling guilty for not doing the chores around the house, I was feeling guilty for ordering food, for not going on a walk, for being in the bathroom too long, for taking a shower… Should I even continue? I was feeling guilty for eating too much or too little. There were no wins. Guilt never left my side. After the babies were born, Twin B had trouble breathing and had to stay in the Neonatal intensive care unit, also known as NICU, for two days. I felt so guilty. I thought it was my fault, even though I had nothing to do with that. He swallowed too much amnionic fluid, but I felt guilt like I had something to do with it. I felt guilty for spending time with Twin A, while my other baby was in the NICU. I felt like a piece of me was missing. I felt like something so crucial was missing, like an arm or my left eye. After the surgery, I wasn't allowed to go see my baby until the nurses give me "an okay," I had to meet certain criteria. I cried, and I begged, but until my body did certain things after my c-section, it wasn't safe for me to go. I was told that since my catheter was out, I had to naturally pee some amount of urine, so I started drinking all the water in the hospital. My bladder was supposed to start working again, but all the liquid that I drank was going in my legs. My legs were swollen, and I mean really swollen. I was so scared to look at them. My feet tripled in size. At one point, I thought that the skin is going to burst. Finally, at 2 AM, I was able to pee naturally. I was feeling guilty that it took me so long to pee a decent amount. Even though I realized that it's not my fault, and it's not my body's fault, this is just what the process is.

Guilt was my unwelcome neighbor. It stayed with me. When in the hospital, nurses asked me if I wanted to give my babies to the nursery so I could get some rest - immediate guilt. "What kind of mother am I, if I literally just gave birth and already handing them out to the nursery?!" And this stupid mentality, "What kind of a mother am I..." just nearly killed me. My babies developed a dairy allergy while on my breastmilk, guilt. When we finally decided to switch them to formula, enormous amount of guilt. And tears. I felt less of a mother. I felt that I wasn't good enough. We had to switch to specialized formula, I cried. I cried a lot. It was getting ridiculous. I was enjoying a meal, while my babies were peacefully sleeping, guilt. It didn't seem ridiculous to me at that time. I was so consumed by my guilt, that logical thoughts did not cross my mind. I didn't realize what was happening, I couldn't look at myself from another perspective, because I was in my mind. Until one day, I started my good old "what kind of a mother I am, if I'm out here eating…." And then it dawned on me. I'm not supposed to eat if I'm a mother? That was a weird realization. Everything was explained to me on my first postpartum appointment at my OB office, guilt is actually a very strong indicator of PPD - Postpartum Depression. She was back. My depression was back.

For the first four months of my children's lives, I cried a lot. At first, I was told it's normal. It's called "baby blues," your hormones are changing, and it's okay to cry, but when I say a lot, I mean every single day, almost every single hour. As I was crying, I was feeling, of course, guilty, because I knew they deserve a better mother. A happy, smiling, full of energy mother. I was not it. I was smiling through tears. When I was playing with my babies, I was crying and I just couldn't help myself. I couldn't stop. My hormones were all over the place. I felt all alone, isolated, with no way out. It was just me. I felt like nobody in the entire world would understand me, because why am I complaining, I was blessed with two amazing, healthy children. What am I whining about? What kind of mother I am? Turned out that all of these big feelings, and all of these big emotions of mine were controlled by my hormones that were out of control trying to adjust after pregnancy. My husband was right beside me through this crazy rollercoaster ride. But no matter how much I explained, no matter how much we talked about everything, there was no way for him to understand me, because he wasn't going through it, I was.

One evening, the babies were just baby-ing, they weren't doing anything extraordinary. Every day, there is something called the "witching hour," all babies experience it. Usually it's from 5-7 PM or somewhere in between, when the baby just cries. For no apparent reason. Just being a baby. Diaper could be changed, they could be fed, all snuggled up and cozy, but something is just happening in their little brains. You can do everything to try and sooth the baby, but nothing works. For us, it was a nightmare. Two babies crying at the same time, crying like something horrible had happened. Crying like they have something terrible happening inside. I was sitting in my kitchen, listening to the crying of the babies, but I couldn't bring myself to go there. My husband was with them, they were perfectly fine. Except, I wasn't. I wasn't fine. I was crying in the kitchen. Thinking that this will never end. Their cry will never stop. I just couldn't handle it. I thought that I'm going crazy, and I can't take it anymore. I have decided to reach out for help. I decided to text a mental health crisis line. I was given this number by my OB office. "If you need support, if you feel like you can't go on, text them, or call them, just reach out." I was told by my doctor. It's a specialized crisis line for people who suffer from postpartum depression. I had no idea it existed. So I did. I texted them.

"Hello?"

It was the first time I used something like this, so I wasn't sure if it's going to be an actual person on the other end, or an automated message. I received a couple of messages about confidentiality and that "messaging rates will apply."

"Hello, my name is Leah, how can I help you today?"

I finally received an answer.

"Are you a real person?" I was just making sure.

"Yes, I'm a licensed psychotherapist. What is your name?"

"My name is Maria."

"What's going on Maria?"

"I'm struggling to put in words my problem. I gave birth via c-section to twins in January. I'm depressed, I have no energy, I'm very tired."

"I hear you, Maria. I am so glad you reached out. We are here to offer brief support and a listening ear. How can I support you today?"

"Honestly, I am not even sure how. I cry a lot. I don't know how to stop it."

"Sometimes, crying can feel good, like a release of stress and sometimes not so much. How are you doing with all the crying you are experiencing?" A green bubble showed up on my screen.

"I feel pretty hopeless. I feel alone. I feel anxious, nervous. I feel like I will never feel like myself again."

"Your body has been through a lot, please give yourself some grace. I had twins 30 years ago. It was no small thing."

"Really? How did you manage the first few months? They are not sleeping. I feel like I'm reliving three hours over and over and over again. I am on autopilot."

"It is so hard. I think it's hard for anyone who has not done it to truly understand. I had a lot of help. Do you have any help?"

"No, it's just me and my husband, we have absolutely no help, and it's our first kids, so we barely know what's going on."

"That's a very common deception for having twins."

"I feel so much guilt. My boys deserve a present mother, but I am all over the place."

"Mom guilt is the worst. I hope you hear me when I say, this is common and your boys will be okay."

I had to go help my husband put the kids to bed, but this conversation gave me what I needed. Just a little bit of clarity, just a little bit of hope. To know, that I'm not alone. To know that I'm not crazy. To know that other women experience it too. It was so important for me. This conversation gave me hope, and I don't even know if Leah really had twins 30 years ago, or she was just trying to connect with me, this gave me hope, and just a little push to keep going.

At my OB appointment, I was prescribed antidepressants. I was pretty much right back where I started. The pills were supposed to start working in a couple of weeks, so I was taking them religiously.

They finally worked. I started to notice the changes in me, I was crying less, I had just a little more energy. I was able to function and see the light. I was relieved to know that it's my hormones, and not my own mind playing tricks on me.

***

If pregnancy was the hardest thing I did physically, postpartum was the hardest thing I did mentally. Postpartum depression goes hand in hand with postpartum anxiety. I was constantly in my thoughts. I had some intrusive thoughts too. Intrusive thoughts were coming to me unexpectedly and made me feel super anxious. I had this horrible image in my mind that one day my babies won't wake up, and I will come up to their crib and see their little faces blue. It was so scary. I also was thinking what if the baby will fall from my arms on the floor head down. What if I accidentally will hit the baby's head on the wall. What if… what if…. These thoughts were very scary. As a mother, to have these thoughts and images in my head, I thought I was going insane, and I had to constantly remind myself that it's not happening, it's all my imagination. This is actually also the reason why we never co-slept with our babies, because I was worried of suffocating one of them, and from there I could never forgive myself. My anxiety was through the roof. My thoughts were racing most of the time and I couldn't stop it. I couldn't stop it even when I really tried. These horrible images would just pop up in my head without my consent. Thankfully, these thoughts went away with antidepressants.

Antidepressants really saved me. I am no longer trapped by these thoughts. Another fear of mine was something called SIDS - sudden infant death syndrome, it's when the baby dies for no reason. I was just numbingly terrified. I had to run away from my thoughts, but I couldn't.

Postpartum also brought rage. I've never in my life experienced anything like it. It's called postpartum rage. When you are so angry that you can't control it. I felt truly horrible for it. For feeling it, and for acting on it. I was so overstimulated that I couldn't control my emotions. Kids are crying, noise from the outside, neighbors are... well, neighbors are just existing, and then... my dog starts barking. My dog, a Frenchie, a cute little innocent creature, I jokingly call him my first born. Oh boy, poor dog. I would scream at him to stop barking. My rage was out of control, but it dialed down when pills started working and I am so thankful. I was so amazed that one little pill per day, can "fix me."

Every symptom "in the book," you name it, I probably had it. I went through a lot, and it really takes a toll on you. All of these mental struggles take away your energy, and at the end of the day, you are just exhausted. On the flip side... the feelings that you have as a mother are like no other. You are exhausted, and sleep deprived, and hungry, and you are tired all the time, but the second you see your little babies... everything lifts. Everything becomes better. It's magical. It's almost like you forget how incredibly tired you are, you forget that you hadn't had a decent night of sleep, you forget that you haven't had a meal in a while, and you stink like a garbage bag. You are a mother now. I am a mother now. I have someone to care for. I have someone more important than anything else in my life. I have someone who depend on me for one hundred percent of the time. I have someone who I love so much I could never imagine. I seriously could never imagine that I can love this deeply. The love you feel for your child is like nothing else in this world. It may come to you right away, or it may take some time, and that's okay. Everybody is different. Either way, what you feel is something truly incredible. I carried you for 37 weeks, I counted your kicks, I cared for you, I ate a ton and drank gallons of water for you to survive, and you are finally here. You are here and I am so grateful. For everything. My pregnancy was not easy, but if I knew that at the end of the road I will have you, my sweet little angels, I would do it all over again, just for you. This love and this bond that you have now is completely unique. You love your husband, you love your parents, your friends, but the way you love your child is unexplainable. Now, only now, I understand what people meant by "just wait." I waited, and look where I am now. I am so deeply and completely in love. I found this new, deeper meaning of love, there is literally nothing else like it. My heart has filled with joy and this overwhelming feeling of fullness. I feel complete now. I feel happy. Maybe for the first time in my life, truly happy.

***

I'm a millennial. I'm an adult, but I feel like there are "real adults" somewhere. There are adults who know how to properly "adult." Does that make sense? When I had my babies, I thought, "Wow, I'm a real grown up now." Now, that it's been some time, I still feel like I'm not "fully adulting." I play with my kids and I get really invested in farting noises, do you know how much fun it is? In all seriousness, everything changes when you have kids. Everything. You change. Your priorities change. You start seeing different perspectives. You no longer have the energy for bullshit. And that's okay. Everything is okay. You don't have to explain yourself to anyone. You really don't. You don't have any other obligations or responsibilities for anyone, except your kids.

When I had my twins, my whole world turned upside down. Not only my relationship with my husband changed, but also with a lot of my friends. I refused to listen to unsolicited advice and judgement from people who don't even have kids. I don't have to. It's hard to realize it and accept it, but once you do, you are free. I felt so uplifted. I felt so free. Most importantly, you don't have to explain yourself to anyone, and it gives you power. As a society, we need to normalize growing apart. We have been normalizing a lot of things, but growing apart as adults needs to be on that list. Growing apart from anyone or anything that does not bring you joy, that does not benefit you or your little family in any way. When it becomes harder and harder to maintain a relationship, normalize ending this relationship. It's okay. If any kind of relationship brings you pain or any type of discomfort - let it go. I did. I let go of a lot of people in my life, good people. Just not my people, I guess. For a brief moment, I felt really lonely, not going to lie. The funniest part of it all, there wasn't a person in my life who actually fought for me to stay. It says a lot. It says a lot about me, but about them also. And guess what? That's okay too. I recently saw a video that said, "Stop texting everybody, disappear for a week, who will be there looking for you?" In my case, there was no one. Nobody was looking for me, nobody was checking up on me, nobody was there for me. It's sad to realize, but it's life. I guess, I wanted more from my friends, I imagined it a little differently. My expectations weren't met, and that's okay. My expectations are my problems, not theirs. Having said that, I also realize that people have lives, but it's not every day your friend brings home twins. It's not every day your friend suffers from depression, it's not every day, and it's not forever. Either way, there will be a lot more people in your life, who will come and go, but the only people who now truly matter, are the people you created from scratch.

Since becoming a mom, I realized that now I'm a "grown up" and I can do anything I want. Literally, anything. Unfortunately, or fortunately, "anything" became limited now. The only things I want now is for some uninterrupted sleep and eat in peace. I used to take these simple pleasures for granted. So yea, I can do anything I want, the only thing that I cannot do now is die. Not on purpose, not by accident. I would probably feel guilty for dying too. I can't die because I want to see my kids every single day. I want to see them grow up; I want to be a part of their lives. I love my kids so much that I can't miss anything that has to do with them. I want to witness all the exciting moments in their lives. Every day brings something new, and I want to be here for it. Now, every time I cross the street, I'm being extra careful. Now, every time I pass by a construction site, I wish nothing falls on my head. A lot of mothers, people, say that they will die for their kids, but the real question is, will you live for your kids? Will you make better choices? Will you keep yourself happy and healthy? Will you go to check out that mole that popped up? Will you finally go for that walk that you said you would so many times? Will you actually live for your kids? Because, I feel like dying for them is easy and of course, if need be you'll do it, but living? Making a conscious decision every day to live, that's the real challenge. Finally quitting your addiction, going on a healthier diet, choosing to live, every single day. I've been thinking about it for a while now, because I was one of those moms who "will kill for my kids, and will die for them," but then I realized that it's too easy. What's not easy is to thrive. To be better, to be healthier. Just to be.

I say "thrive" like it's nothing, but in reality, in motherhood, there are a lot of days of pure survival. There are a lot of days when everything goes wrong. There are a lot of days where you don't feel like you're being and doing your best. It's important to remember that these days pass. Nothing is forever. It may not seem like much, but these days teach us that we are human. Good days become bad days, bad days become good days, and it's a wild rollercoaster. Nothing is forever. The newborn stage ends, and the fog lifts, and you find your voice again. Then comes infant stage with its own challenges. That passes too.

Then goes the baby stage, and you already feel completely different from where you started. After the baby phase, here goes the toddler stage and you come alive. It's like you shed your skin and you reborn. Every stage is hard, but you take it one day at a time and they pass so fast. Every phase brings its own hardships and fears. In the newborn stage, I was so sleep deprived that every time I fell asleep, I woke up sweating and asking "Where is the baby?"

I was so afraid to fall asleep with baby in my hands and crush it with my body. While in infant stage, I was constantly looking for milestones that babies are supposed to "meet." I had such fear of them not succeeding, and not meeting the goals, and "guidelines." Right before they turned one, I was really up in their business, looking at their teeth and counting, "Is this a tooth? How many teeth they got? Is it enough? Is it supposed to be like that?"

I was constantly so worried. I was looking for signs of autism. I think all moms go through it, every day, looking for "signs of autism." All of this is exhausting. Constantly worrying, constantly looking for something, and honestly, you don't even know what you are looking for. I had to always remind myself that all babies develop differently, and if your six month old is not washing the dishes yet, that's okay. Listen, they will at one point. I had to always remember, and trust myself, and our pediatrician. Your baby's doctor will let you know if anything is wrong, so choose wisely.

Everything changes when you have kids. Absolutely everything. Most importantly, you change. You start your life all over again. There is a very interesting animal fact that really put everything in perspective for me. Flamingoes are usually pink, they get their color from eating a lot of shrimp, but when a female flamingo gives birth, they lose their pink. For the first year of carrying for their baby, they lose their pink and they become pale, because of how hard it is to take care of a child. They get it back after a while, but people lose their pink too. Mothers lose their pink. I don't know when I will get my pink back, but I know I'm headed in that direction. Finding yourself in motherhood is very challenging, because you really have no time nor the energy to sit and figure everything out. I know that one day, I will have my pink back, even prettier and brighter than before, but for now, I just have to survive. One day at a time.

***

When my twins were about 4 months old, we were on the edge. Imagine sleeping just a few hours per day, and then all day long take care of two crying babies. Changing, feeding, entertaining, burping, and everything that comes with it. Over and over again. I was depressed and my husband was a walking shell of a person, we were so desperate for some sleep, and peace, that we have decided to sleep train. First of all, let me clarify something, sleep and babies do not mix. It's very hard for them. For some reason, sleep is not something that comes naturally. Babies have to be taught how to sleep. A lot of the babies have something called day and night confusion. They can sleep during the day, but at night, it's party time. A lot of babies can't fall asleep on their own, and you supposed to rock them to sleep all the time. There is a lot that's going on. Having twins, we really didn't have much options but to sleep train. I only have two hands, who do I rock to sleep? How do I do it simultaneously? My husband is not always going to be there to help me put them to sleep. There are a lot of sleep training options, and each family can decide for themselves, what works best for them. There are four major sleep training techniques: The Ferber method, cry it out, fading method and chair method. We chose "cry it out," although, after researching it more carefully, we actually did the Ferber method. Ferber method is when your baby starts crying, you wait 3-5 minutes, then you go in and check on them, you reassure them that everything is okay, and you leave. Cry it out method is when you just leave your baby to cry themselves to sleep. The purpose of all these methods is to teach your child how to self-soothe. The fading method is when you stay in your child's room until they fall asleep. And the chair method is when you sit by their crib in a chair, and each night the chair moves further and further away from the crib, until you leave the room. We were so sleep deprived that there was no time for research, we needed sleep right now. Cry it out method is proven to be the fastest way to teach your kid to sleep.

Oh boy… when I tell you how hard it was. It is so incredibly painful to hear your child crying. It is almost unbearable. They were crying, and I was crying too. I wanted to run in there, and pick them up and tell them that everything is okay, and I'm here, but who do I pick up? How do I choose between my two babies? That's a very big dilemma of parents with multiples. We lived in a one bedroom apartment and there was no running away from their crying. No running away, until… until we bought two bassinets, the cheapest ones, and put them in the kitchen. My husband stayed in the living room to monitor them over night, and I slept in the bedroom. We read that cry it out method will work in 3-4 days. We patiently waited. Day one they cried for an hour and a half. My husband would come in, and check on them and leave them be. Second day, third day, fourth day, the crying would fade away, but it was still a lot. They weren't sleeping longer stretches, forget about sleeping through the night. We tried and tried again, it wasn't working. After all, I said that's enough, and we came back to feeding them at night.

Honestly, I think we tried everything. Feeding them, not feeding them, rocking them, not rocking them, leaving them to cry, attending to them, nothing was working. It was a very hard road. Swaddling them, not swaddling them, pacifier, no pacifier, there was no sleep in our house. I saw videos of people getting some sort of sleep suits, so I ordered it for them, and I had high hopes for it. The first night we tried it, I was so hopeful for some good amount of sleep, but that did not work either. It seemed endless, and I thought that my babies will just not sleep ever. I thought that we will never sleep again and this is our new reality. You get used to it, motherhood showed me that you get used to everything, pretty much. You learn how to "sleep on demand," you learn to wake up after just an hour of rest, and you go on, because there is no other solution. You learn to wake up in the middle of the night, you train yourself. My babies slept through the night for the first time ever when they were about 8 months old.

My twins also had something called day and night confusion. During the day they were tired, and it was impossible for me to keep them awake, they slept like they are supposed to, but at night... I had a fear of night. There is something about the quietness of the night. It's like the world stops. It's like nobody else exists. It's only you. You and your child. It is romanticized a lot, people are saying that when you feel all alone at night, and it feels like nobody else is awake, there is another mother, rocking her child to sleep. Just like you. But in reality, you are on autopilot. Your child wakes up, and you panicking thinking what could it be? Diaper? Food? Pain? Bad dream? And you get up and start doing all the things to get him to go back to sleep, so you could go back to sleep, because you are totally and absolutely exhausted. And it happens over and over and over again, until you think that you can't do this anymore, but let me tell you.... You can. You can do this and you do it. You do it every single night up until they don't need you anymore. It is bitter sweet. You get so used to it. You get used to everything. Some people get lucky and their children start sleeping through the night at 8-10 weeks old. But some people, like me, haven't slept in 8 months now, and by the time my children slept through the night for the first time, I fucked up my sleep so much so that I was waking up at 3 am even if both of my kids were sleeping. So yea, mothers are superior. Women are incredible.

The quietness of the night... some nights I really needed it. Some days were super hard, and with everything going on, I needed the noise to stop. I needed peace. The mental load that you carry with you every day, sometimes is unbearable. You keep in mind every little thing and it exhausts you. The city gets quiet, and you feel completely alone. You feel like there is nobody else awake. You feel like you are the only person on this planet. You start dreading evenings, and start to procrastinate their bedtime, because you already know that the night is coming. It made me feel better to think about other moms out there. Other moms who are also not sleeping, and rocking their babies. It gave me a peace of mind to know that I'm not alone. Then you get this sense of relief when you see the sunrise. You hear some cars outside, and you know that you have survived yet another night. For those who say "sleep when the baby sleeps," I will always answer, "yes, and do the dishes when the baby does the dishes, and do the laundry when the baby does the laundry," it's a funny story. You get the point. In my mind, I was missing the "normalcy" of my life, because I had no idea what's going to happen tomorrow.

My advice, sleep when the baby sleeps, but do everything you need to do when the babies are awake. Don't leave everything for their nap time. When the babies are sleeping, and you get this quietness in the house, you rest. Do whatever you want, sleep, or scroll on your phone, or read a book, whatever brings you joy. Only this way you can take back the control. Before you know it, they will be awake again, and you supposed to do everything all over again. I did not realize it from the beginning how crucially important it is to take care of yourself. It is, trust me, the most important thing for your family, for you to take care of yourself. During that time, I was feeling like I'm fading away. I did not take care of myself, even my basic needs. I couldn't even eat normally when the babies were crying, because I thought that I had to attend to them right away, this second. I would put my meal on pause, and then forget about it all together. That's why I lost almost 70 pounds in two months, because I didn't take care of myself. I couldn't trust anybody with my babies, and I had the hardest time dedicating chores around the house. I thought I could do it all alone, all by myself, everything, but you can't. It's important to realize it sooner rather than later, you cannot do everything by yourself.

One day, my husband said, "This Friday, is your day off. Get some wine, think about what you want to do, and do whatever you want."

I was really excited, but I also was really nervous. I was already hooked and fully addicted to my babies. What do you mean "day off"? Mothers don't get a day off. If you think about it, you never saw your mom sick when you were little, that's not because she was never sick, it's because there was no time to be sick. I was patiently waiting for my Friday. I got everything ready, Grey's Anatomy new season, wine chilling in the fridge, my face-masks. Finally the day was here. My husband was closed off with the babies in the bedroom and I had the rest of the apartment to myself. I didn't have to react to the babies' cries, or worry about changing their diapers. To tell you the truth, watching an episode of your favorite show uninterrupted makes all the difference. I was drinking my wine, with a face mask on, watching Grey's Anatomy and it was great, everything was perfect, except that I couldn't relax. I was constantly thinking that something might go wrong. What if something happens? What if I had to drive? What if I have to do something for the babies? I was always on full alert. My mind flooded with unpredictable scenarios. I started thinking, "What if we have to go to the emergency room, and here I am with a face mask on and smelling like wine?"

I washed off my mask pretty fast. Every time the babies cried, I wanted to run in the room and to the rescue, but my husband did not "allow" me, because it was my day off, and I had to learn again, to relax.

It's been a while, and it's gotten better, but I have yet to learn how to relax. I know that it's extremely important to unwind. But my mind is always, always, always with my babies. Not only my mind, honestly, my whole body is with my babies. My anxiety doesn't allow me to fully relax and be in the moment. Since my first "day off," I had a couple opportunities to "relax," but every time, I fail. It's hard to think about yourself when you have two human beings that completely depend on you 24/7. These two little humans are thieves, they stole my heart. They will be keeping my heart hostage for the rest of my life. And I'm okay with that, because I am so completely in love with my babies. One day, I will learn again how to relax and one day, I will rest, just not right now. Just not yet.

***

"Misery loves company" I learned it so fast. While I was on the "night shift" with my babies, one of them wasn't sleeping, and I was sitting in the dark room, trying not to wake up the second twin. Trying to calm my baby down, my back was killing me and all of a sudden, the door opens, and my husband walks in. At that moment it was like the air that I desperately needed. Seeing that I'm not alone, and feeling not alone at that moment is what I really needed to keep going.

In the newborn stage, when babies were waking up at night to eat, I was panicking, because I couldn't feed them both at once, so I had to do it one by one. That meant that while the first baby eats, the second one is screaming bloody murder. I was so alert, and so aware of the noise and their cries, it made me feel miserable, and so scared. But once in a while, that bedroom door opened, and my husband walked in to feed the second child. I learned that misery really does love company, it's true. When you see that you are not alone battling two crying babies, it feels amazing. Same thing happened when my babies started teething. I could only sooth one baby at a time, but just when I was starting to feel defeated, that door opened. We were both standing there, in complete darkness, rocking our children, trying to calm them down. That's why when I say that your partner matters, your partner really matters so much. It's not only about the night feedings and teething, when every day I'm by myself taking care of my twins I feel on edge. My cortisol levels are through the roof, because of all the responsibilities. When you are the default parent, there is so much going on in your mind, it's hard to let go. As soon as that door opens and my husband walks through it, I feel immediate relief. I have a back up now, I'm not alone. As soon as I hear keys in that lock, my heart jumps and my mood is uplifted that very second.

Being the "default parent" means keeping everything in check. Feeding schedule and the menu, preparing the food, keeping up with doctors' appointments, ordering diapers and wipes, sleeping schedule, toy rotation, entertainment of the babies, God forbid sickness, and all the rest of it. It's hard when you realize that your mind is always busy. I remember in the hospital, once I had the twins, nurse handed me a folder with a bunch of papers in it. I didn't pay too much attention to it, because, well, two babies. It turned out that those papers were super important, it was the birth certificate forms for my children. So after all the procedures and all the drugs that I was on, I had to fill out the forms. To be honest, I don't remember how I did that. I had to gather my thoughts together, I had to put my mind to it, because I couldn't mess up on these very important documents. Also, nobody told me, but you supposed to have a pediatrician "on standby". I had to call my insurance to put my babies on. I had to schedule that pediatrician's appointment, because I was told that I can't be discharged from the hospital if I have no appointment. Everything was happening so fast. I was in the hospital, trying to wrap my head around of what just happened, but there was no time to waste. I had to do what I had to do.

I guess it was true when everybody told me "enjoy the calm before the babies get here". It was really hard to enjoy the pain though, but overall, there is truly no calm after the twins were born. Everything was a blur. In the hospital, a lot is going on actually. Everybody is checking on you every 20 minutes, the bed is moving to prevent blood clots, it was impossible to sleep, you supposed to order food at a certain hour, nurses, doctors, babies, everything is happening so fast. But... I was so high on the adrenaline, well, and the drugs they had me on, but adrenaline was taking over. It truly felt like my life has officially just started. It's a weird feeling. I was overwhelmed, but at the same time, so excited. I was excited to be with my children. I caught myself thinking: "I want to go home, because I want to undress my kids and just look at everything, remember their little toes, and their little fingers. I want to kiss them and hug them and not be interrupted even for a second" I couldn't wait to go home and "start my life".

It was funny how in the hospital I had no idea what to do with my babies and nurses were showing me how to change them, and feed them, and how to swaddle them and at that moment I felt like everything was under control, I got this. When I was left alone, the babies started crying, and I panicked. "Is your diaper wet? Are you hungry? Why are you crying?" Only later I learned that babies just cry sometimes, it's their only job. One time I was struggling to sooth the babies, and I was pressing on the "call button" for someone to come to my rescue, but all the nurses were busy. I was a wreck. I started doing everything, changing the diaper, feeding, rocking, but it's two babies, and I couldn't hold them both at the same time. I was going nuts. I slowly wobbled to the hall, and asked for someone to help me, and a nurse came by. Turns out one of the very first poops for tiny humans are sometimes challenging. She took care of that for me, and I was so grateful. Everything was once again, under control, except for me. I was not. They called it "baby blues".

***

"Baby blues"… Here is something interesting. I had no idea this is happening to a woman once she gives birth. My hormones were adjusting, and I got this very strong urge to cry. It's a very drastic change in your body, once you give birth, the hormones are going crazy, that's why it happens. Everybody told me it was normal. And yet, a social worker came by my room to check if I was okay. I did not yet realize anything at that point, it was my second day at the hospital. I was crying, all the time. All the time. I was looking at my babies, and crying. I am a mother now. Was I crying because I was starting to realize what just happened? Was I crying because I thought about something and it made me emotional? No. It was all just happening for no reason.

I was crying for a while, first month, second month, until I realized that it's not "baby blues" anymore, it's my mental health. I was spiraling out of control. The one constant question I had was: "when does it get easier?" I had to wait for that answer. It got a little easier after one year. But every stage comes with its own challenges.

After my twins turned one, the darkness lifted a little. I was able to breath just a little more. Thankfully, or unfortunately, the time does not stay still. Babies grow and develop into these beautiful, amazing human beings. After one year they started consistently sleeping through the night. After one year, they started to understand more and more of what I was saying to them. They were able to bring me their toys, they were able to take their first steps. They started mumbling something completely non-sensical, but with all the seriousness in their little faces. It's adorable. After one whole year we found our "normalcy" again. We found our routine. And this whole year, I kept on asking this question, when does it get easier. What I had to do is wait. Wait again.

That first year is like a blurry painting. I know it was beautiful, because I created it myself, but I can't pin point what was beautiful about it. Everything was new for me, for my husband, and for my kids. We were all just taking it day by day, trying to figure it all out together. After the first year, you have a little more freedom. Babies already eating solid food and start to taste different stuff, they start drinking whole milk, which was such a relief. Our specialized formula we had to find in the pharmacies, but milk, you can just buy at the store, and never have to worry about running out. Once again, I am so happy that I took millions and millions of videos and pictures, because now, looking back at everything, I remember… I remember it all. I remember how incredibly hard it was, and I smile, because we made it. We came out on top.

That first year was super task, to be honest. As much as it was eventful and joyful, it was so hard. That brought me to my next question: "why this happiness is so hard to achieve? Why does it have to be so freaking hard?" They say "rainbow comes after the rain", but it was always raining, and I know it was mostly because of my mental state. I was battling a postpartum depression. It was almost impossible for me to see the light, thankfully, I got out. The rainbow is here, and the light that I see right now, couldn't be any brighter.

I talk a lot about how difficult it is raising children, but it's because nobody else does. Social media is a lie. With that being said, I want to emphasis how amazing it is to watch them grow. Each step they take, every milestone they hit is pure magic. Every little thing that they achieve is my own personal form of payment. Since there is no communication for a long while, and you are left guessing if you're doing everything right, every little thing that my kids learn is considered as payment and reassurance to me. I guess, I'm doing something right, and it feels really good to realize it.

Accepting that I have postpartum depression wasn't hard for me, because I was desperate for an explanation for why I'm feeling the way I'm feeling. Depression made perfect sense and I was not crazy. It was so important for me to know that I'm not crazy. Once again, looking at social media, and seeing how other women handle postpartum, raised a lot of questions for me. "What is wrong with me?" was one of the questions I constantly asked myself. "What the hell is wrong with me?" The answer is nothing. Nothing is "wrong" with me. It was just my journey. I had to go through what I went through in order to be stronger.

I don't know if God exists, but I know now that this challenge was given to me to show me how strong I am. It's kind of funny, because I am already pretty strong, and I'm not trying to be Hulk. I guess I was given this opportunity to see myself in different light, to see what I'm capable of. I don't know if God exists, but I thank him and the universe for allowing me to experience everything that I've been through.

***

For the first year of my twins, I was in survival mode so much, that I was afraid to forget everything. My mind was so foggy and busy all the time. So to solve this problem, I wanted to make something meaningful, something forever. I started printing tons of pictures. I printed a lot. I got all sorts of photo albums and cute little things. I made a little notebook so I can keep track of everything. I know I could've bought a special notebook for this, there is a bunch of them on the market, but I've decided to make my own. I started a notebook, glued in some pictures, bought some cute stickers, and started sort of a diary for my kids. Every progress they make, every little step they take, I wrote it all down, with dates and details. First time they rolled over, first steps, first blow out diaper, everything was documented. All the songs that I made up for them, I wrote it all down. That was also my attempt to take control of the situation, because when I see it on paper, it becomes real. In my mind, I want to give this notebook to my twins when they turn 18 years old. Yes, I'm thinking that far ahead. It's been some time now, and I'm still filling out the pages of that notebook, because I want to remember every little thing.

I was cleaning out their closet, and I found their swaddles. I remembered those late nights when we used to swaddle the babies, they looked like the most delicious burritos. I couldn't throw it away. I carefully folded the swaddles and put it back in the closet. This happens often, I avoid throwing away those little keepsakes. I don't have this much room in the apartment, but what can I do? Throw it away? Nonsense! Whether I have good or bad memories, I'm a sentimental mom. I was always a sentimental person, but I thought that I would want to forget the hard times… Turns out, even those incredibly difficult times shaped me into a person, a mother I am today. I even kept one diaper of each size that we went through, and now, looking back at the newborn diaper, seems so surreal that my babies were ever this little. Time got away from me, but at the same time, it was like yesterday. It seems like I vividly remember everything, but it's not true. My mind plays a trick on me. My mind is trying to get me pregnant again. Ha-ha. In all seriousness, I can't go through everything again.

During the very first year of raising my twins, I longed to be in a community. I needed to know that I'm not alone. But there was no one. I was absolutely alone. That's why all the mom's blogs and mom's forums are so popular. I watched videos of other moms constantly comparing myself to them. Mothers' community is very strong, once you find your crowd. It's very united. I have not met another mother who was rude to me. One time I went to the store and on my way back I saw three women with strollers. I got really nervous, because I wanted to ask them some questions. I worked up the courage and awkwardly walked up to them.

"Hi, sorry for the bother, I'm a new mom to twins and I wanted to ask you guys something."

"Sure, what's up?" These women asked.

"How do I get them to sleep through the night? They are 5 months old, and it seems like an impossible task." I was standing in front of these women, feeling like a child myself, asking some ridiculous questions, it seemed so desperate. And that's because I was. I was desperate. I was desperate for answers, but also for some simple human interaction.

"That's a hard question. They should sleep through the night by the time they go to college." Everybody started laughing. I laughed as well, but at the time, I did not find it that funny. I was sleep deprived and in need of some reassurance.

"They will sleep when they are ready to sleep, there is nothing really that you can do." One of the ladies said. "My oldest started sleeping around 15 months, my second one still waking up for a bottle at 18 months." She smiled. I got visibly upset, because I thought that with twins, I will never sleep again. At that stage, I needed my sleep back. I was really desperate. These ladies did not really make me feel any better. After I got home, I was thinking that I will never talk to anyone ever again, because everything I hear upsets me. As time went on, I met other people, other mothers, who, in fact, reassured me, that kids will sleep. Soon. They will sleep soon. I waited. Now, writing this makes me laugh, because imagine a girl walking around the neighborhood, looking like a zombie, asking when kids will sleep. That's so funny.

I wonder if all the moms go through this. You want to remember the smallest things about your children, but at the same time, you want to forget the moments that brought you so much mental and physical pain. I wonder if all the mothers struggling the same. I wonder if all the moms are going through so much. And if so, why isn't anyone screaming about their experience? It's like we all collectively agreed that only when you have a child, you shall understand...

***

From all the interactions that I had with other women, during my pregnancy and after, one conversation stands out. One time, me and my husband took the kids to the park. It was an incredibly hot day in New York. We decided to go to the swings. The park was pretty empty, because the weather was brutal. We came up to the swings and took the kids out of the stroller. I wiped off the seat of the swings to cool it off a little. There was an older lady right beside us. She had like five kids of different ages with her. She was starring at us. After a couple of minutes, she asked: "Are those twins?"

"Yes" We replied.

She started smiling and continued talking.

"You got your hands full!"

Me and my husband were awkwardly smiling and nodding our heads.

"I have eleven children" she said.

"Looks like you are the one whose hands are full!" We laughed.

"Oh yes, I have all ages too! My oldest one just got married not too long ago, and I'm going to be a grandma soon!"

"Congratulations! That's so exciting! Any advice you can give us?"

The lady started smiling from ear to ear. It was like we were speaking her language.

"Yes! Enjoy them! Before you know it, they will grow up. Enjoy them while they are little! You blink, and they don't need you anymore."

I guess I'm blinking incorrectly.

"It's hard to enjoy because we are constantly exhausted, unfortunately."

"You guys don't have any help?"

"We don't."

"Oh no, that's not good! It takes a village to raise even one child, and you have two at the same time!"

"Yep, we don't have a village, it's just the two of us."

"It's going to get easier. Don't worry! Just try to enjoy them."

While standing there talking to her, one of my kids was having a blast on the swings, the other one, not so much. We talked for a couple of minutes and left the park. Me and my husband were talking and came to realization that we really do have it hard. We don't have the luxury of relaxing or even being alone with each other. It's always about the kids. Our conversations are mostly about the kids. Our thoughts and what we do on a day-to-day basis are about our boys. People who have help, nannies or relatives, will never understand. When you have no one to rely on, when you have no other options, but to get up and do. Do what needs to be done. Every single day. It's truly a game you play on a hard level. It's an extreme sport.

My mind is simply exhausted from the responsibilities and the pressure all the time. There are no weekends, no days off. At absolutely all times, it's just me and my husband. When one of us is sick, the other one has to step up. All the time. My mind has no breaks, nor does my husband. There is nobody else to rely on, in an emergency situation, or even the everyday life. As much as we try to enjoy our children, the fatigue is real. It takes a toll on you.

A very important conversation to have is the one where you decide what happens to your children if, God forbid, anything happens to you, parents. Unfortunately, I have no idea. It bothers me. Our conversation ended with a decision that nothing can ever happen to us. We should just be extra careful. Oh, the uncertainty. All of these important decisions drain you. As a parent, you are literally responsible for everything. You are literally responsibly for the life of your little one, but also for your own life. This really keeps you on your toes, if you think about it. I went through life without giving it a second thought, but now I can't. It's crazy. As much as I'm trying to enjoy my lids and be in the moment, there is always something on the back of my mind. And this "something" is always important. There is really no "chill time" for me. This makes me wonder, once again, do all women go through this? Is it the same for everyone? Or is it just me and my anxiety against the world? I mentioned earlier that mom's community is very strong, but as soon as you start asking questions, everybody has everything under control. How weird is this? Nobody is panicking. Looks like everybody knows what they are doing. Nobody has any problems, or is ever tired, nobody is in distress.

It was a big reason why I've decided to write this book. To open eyes. To open the eyes of people, women on parenthood. It is so important to understand how hard everything is. A child is a huge responsibility and it's not just fun and games all the time. At the same time, I don't want to scare anybody. Really. It's just my experience. Every family has a different experience and I realize that. Overall, I agree with that lady, it's important to enjoy your kids, but sometimes it seems almost impossible. And you know what? That's okay. It's okay to whine and complain. It's okay to acknowledge how hard raising a child is. It's okay to be tired. It's okay to speak your mind. This seriously needs to be normalized.

I enjoy my kids, at least I really, truly try. They are the best thing that ever happened to me. At the same time, I just want to spread awareness about the hardships that a child brings. Every time you play with your baby, it is one of a kind feeling. Every time your child learns something new, you feel so much pride. Every time your kid does something new, it's an unbelievable feeling of warmth. But this happiness is hard to maintain, and it's totally okay to admit that

***

A lot of people talk about pregnancy cravings. There are a lot of things that pregnant women might want. Some people have weird cravings, but at the time, it doesn't seem weird at all. Some women crave salt, some crave sugar, or sweets in general, or it can even be chalk or not food items at all. I didn't have any weird cravings. I honestly don't remember having any cravings at all, except for maybe salt and vinegar chips. I just craved food. I wanted to eat and never stop eating. At the very beginning I ate chips, and in my third trimester I wanted Tums, because the heartburn was no joke. It was brutal. I think I had heartburn just because I breathed air, and drank water.

There was something that crowded my mind though. I have been smoking cigarettes for as long as I can remember myself. Once we started trying for a baby, I quit. I quit and never looked back. No questions asked, I quit right away, because I couldn't risk the health of my child, just because I have a weak will power. But the thought of having a cigarette was pretty strong. That was my biggest craving during my pregnancy. Cigarette and salt and vinegar chips. I also sometimes wanted a Red Bull, but that wasn't as strong.

Once I gave birth, I couldn't wait to get back to "normal" life. There was no "normal" anymore. I was still deeply connected to my babies because I was breastfeeding. I couldn't wait to get myself back, to get my body back. Turns out that when you give birth, you still cannot do a lot of things if you are breastfeeding. One of those things, I found out the hard way, I ate some pea soup, and my babies had the worst gas and colic ever, so yea, you can't "go back to normal" after birth. At my first OB appointment after birth, I worked up the courage and finally asked if I can have just one, tiny, little cigarette. A lot of people and doctors talk about having alcohol after birth, but nobody ever mentions cigarettes. I wasn't craving alcohol, I was craving that first, fresh pull. I saw it in my dreams, I imagined what it would feel like. My OB gave me a "okay" to have a cigarette, as long as it's going to be 3-4 hours between pumping. Nicotine goes into your bloodstream and then into your breastmilk. After the appointment, I was pretty excited. I already anticipated my cigarette. I went to the store and bought one single cigarette, a Lucy. I carefully placed it in my wallet, so it wouldn't break.

At night, when we put the kids to bed "for the night," I started pumping. I was pumping like I never pumped before. I was looking forward to my reward. I pumped for extra 10 minutes, just to be on the safe side. After which, I immediately took my cigarette, lighter, and went outside. I didn't pump during the night, so I was free until about 4-5 in the morning. I came downstairs and breathed in the fresh, crisp, cold air of February. I finally lit up my cigarette. That very first pull was out of this world. It was so refreshing. After so many months of not smoking, I got really lightheaded. But it was so worth it. I was standing outside of my building, feeling "normal," for the first time in so long. That cigarette and that feeling of freedom will stay with me forever, I think.

I wish that I would crave something healthier, because craving smoking is not something I'm proud of. It's the harsh truth. Women, as adults, make all sorts of decisions, and my decision was to smoke during my adult years. I take full responsibility for that. What I am proud of though, is that I was able to put my habit on pause, for the sake of my kids. Motherhood, summed up, is a sacrifice, but it's a sacrifice that you are willing to make and happily do it, because all you can think about is your child.

***

In my life, I always coped with problems by running. Whether it was physically walking away, or numbing my feeling by going out. I also always loved writing. I feel like paper can take anything. Paper will forever forgive me. Paper will patiently listen. Paper won't judge. When something in my life happened, I always wrote it down. Always. I expressed my feelings on paper, because paper doesn't talk back. It was my coping mechanism through all of my struggles in life.

One day, I was sitting in my kitchen, I sit there often, and an epiphany downed on me. I grabbed a piece of envelope that was laying on the table, it had my gas bill in it, and started writing:

"Love is not death. Love is not a sacrifice. Love is not reproaches and humiliation. Love does not fight and scream. Love is not something you can say in a couple of words. Love can be silent. Love is life. Love is a choice. Love is warmth and happiness. Love is immense. Love is deeper than the ocean. But that's love in general. The love for your child... Love for your child is endless. Love for your child is support, not meaningless hugs, not empty words. You can't see love, you can't touch it, you can only feel it. You can feel it somewhere deep inside of your heart, a part of your heart that you never knew existed, before you had a child. Love doesn't have to be earned. It doesn't have to be achieved. Love for your child comes so easy, so effortlessly. Your kid just exists, and you love him no matter what. No matter the circumstances. Love for your child can not disappear, because mothers' heart will always heal itself, because it's love. Love heals, love inspires."

My children inspired me to write, again. Again and again. Through all of the ups and downs, I wrote through it. Through all my struggles during pregnancy, during motherhood, I was writing. I was writing even when I was so down, I couldn't even keep my head straight. I pulled through. I pulled through because of the antidepressants, but also, because I was writing. This book was made possible because of my depression, but also, because of my children who push me to be better every single day.

Motherhood is tricky. One day you are feeling like you've got this, and everything is under control. The other day you could be feeling like everything is falling apart, and you are falling apart as well. It's important to remember that everything ends. The bad days end, the good days end also. Nothing is forever. Before you know it, the colic and gas stage will pass, and your kids are running free in the park. Before you know it, they are going to school. The trick is to try and enjoy every moment. Even though it's hard. It's hard to enjoy when you are surviving and then you feel guilty for not being present. Motherhood is tricky. But remember: "the days are long, but the years are short."

One night, twin A was waking up pretty frequently. Twins went to sleep at 7 pm, and at 9 pm I heard a loud cry, which was unusual. By 6 months, we have "trained" the twins to sleep longer stretches during the night, until the feeding, at around 2 am. Twin A woke up at 9 pm and was crying. My husband was trying to calm him down, but nothing was working. I went in the room, and took him. I rocked him for a while. I took him in my arms and tried to settle him down. He stopped crying. He put his little head on my shoulder, started sucking on his thumb and drifted off to sleep. I held him for a little bit and put him back in his crib. That night, my husband opened my eyes on something, he said, "Do you feel like a mother yet? He calmed down after you took him. He felt you. He smelled you. He knows he is safe."

After those words, I felt so good. I was tired as shit, but I was so happy. And that's what motherhood is mostly about.

None of the "what to expect when you're expecting" books can prepare you for what you are about to experience. Every child is different, every journey is different. It's kind of shocking how many times I told myself, "I can't do this anymore. I can't do it. I just can't."

And then you do it. You do it no matter what. You do it every single day. You do it even if you don't want to. You do it even when you are sick, and tired. You just do it. You do it all. Over and over and over again. Motherhood is the absolute hardest thing that I have personally done in my entire life. You are so incredibly tired all the time, that you don't have your own thoughts anymore. You are completely exhausted at all times of the day and night. Whenever you get a second of free time, you immediately start thinking, "What did I forget to do?"

You wait for the bedtime routine, to finally get some fresh air, and the second your babies go to sleep, you start missing them. Motherhood is weird. It's a rocky road, but the views are amazing.

***

You are sitting in your kitchen. With a glass of your favorite wine. And your dog is barking like crazy, but you don't care. You don't care because you are completely in a different space. You are not there. You get a sniff of a cigarette smell, and you reminisce. You used to smoke. That cigarette smell is what has been left. That cigarette smell reminds you of who you used to be. Or maybe who you still are?

But you're not. The wind blows into your apartment, through an open window in your kitchen where you are, and you get this strong smell of a men's cologne. You used to hang out at bars and clubs. Everybody had that cologne. It's probably 2015, 2016. That cologne was on everybody. You sit in your kitchen and you think about all the things. All the things that you did. And all the things that's left to do. You have your third glass of wine. And you start to notice how you changed. You changed a lot but not at all. Not at all if you really think about it. You are still the same person, but you are completely different. You don't understand it, nobody does. And you are lost, within yourself.

You are in a constant waiting mode. Considering that I hate waiting, I was tortured. You want it to be over, but at the same time you are so fascinated with the outcome. I'm talking about pregnancy, of course, but the rest of it too. Once I got my babies, I was so tired at all times that I wanted to get away. I wanted just a little bit of time for myself, and when I finally got the time, I had no idea what to do with myself. I was devastated to find out that I completely lost myself. I was sitting by Central Park, waiting for my friend, and was just lost. Within myself. It's like I have forgotten who I am. I forgot how to be with myself. What do I like? What should I think about? Is there anything I should be doing? My thoughts were flooded with my kids, my husband, my family, but not me. I have been lost. I lost myself in motherhood. I have forgotten who I am.

I was on a new path to find me. Who am I? My body. My body was not mine anymore. I have grown two human beings and have completely dissolved in them. My body has changed drastically. My body is so different that I don't even recognize it any more. All the physical changes yes, but also the inside, literally. The stretch marks, the loose skin, the pigmentations, the slight color change, freckles, pimples, all the rest of it. But inside…. After my c-section, I felt like all my organs were upside down. I felt completely different. I was feeling hunger differently, I was feeling fullness differently. Everything inside of me changed. I changed. I changed. I changed. And I have yet to accept the new me. I have to get to know the new me. Who am I? Outside of being a new mom, I'm still myself. Or am I? Is being a mom now the most important? Or should I be looking for this new version of me? Outside of being a mom. I walk outside and people don't know that I'm a mom of twins. People see me as a separate person. Who is this person? Is she happy? Is she sad? Is she angry? Is she hungry? I have no idea.

How do I find myself? How do I find out who I am? Is there a questionnaire to figure these things out? I am so unsure of everything. It's definitely a struggle for me. I was so lost in this new version of myself, that I have not recognized my needs as a person, not as a mother, but as a separate person. I know that I'm not alone in this. A lot of mothers get lost in motherhood and try to find themselves. This is where the "new pink" comes in. You supposed to find your new pink, and you supposed to shine brighter than the sun itself. It doesn't happen this easily. It doesn't happen for a long time. So you wait. You wait until you get your pink back, until you get your shine back. I'm still waiting. It's important to not lose hope, and to see what comes next. You wait until you get your head straight, you just wait. Pregnancy, motherhood, and all that it entails, is a big waiting game. Let's just hope I don't lose.

***

Looking back at my fourth trimester, the 12 weeks after I gave birth, what could have helped me? Maybe something could've prevented me from getting my depression? I honestly don't think anything could've prevented it, but maybe some things could have made it better for me. I would recommend myself getting into the shower every single day. Whether it's a 20 minutes shower, or just a 5 minute shower, just get in there. Let me tell you, shower after the hospital hit different. There is something about feeling clean and being refreshed. I did not do it while in my fourth trimester. I was just so out of it. My energy levels were so low, I could only shower every three-four days. Considering your hormones are changing, just imagine the stink. After you give birth, your body starts producing "extra stink" so it's easier for the baby to find you. Even though, it's not like you're playing hide-and-seek with the baby, you are always right there. I went to my OB and she was checking my breast for mastitis, and I had to lift up my arms, because your milk is actually produced not only in your breast, but in your underarm glands; and Oh my God! The stink! I started apologizing to the doctor, but she explained to me that everything is okay, and it's absolutely normal. With that being said, I recommend getting into the shower every day not only for hygiene, but for your mental health. There is something about a shower after birth. There is something about water that cleanses you of all the negative thoughts. Just get into the shower, you will feel better.

The second thing I would recommend is getting outside. Getting outside is so important. Whether it's going for a walk with your little one, or just you alone; just go. Get out. Look at other people, show yourself, and remind yourself that there is life outside of your four walls. Fresh air, sun in your hair, just get outside. I did not. And it cost me. It cost me my mental health. I did not get out of the house for multiple reasons. First, being after a c-section, it was hard for me to move in general. We lived in the building where I had to take the stairs, and after the surgery it was almost impossible for me to do. Second of all, the babies were born in January, when the temperatures outside were hitting pretty low. We were just afraid for the babies. At one time, my husband had to get back to work, and I was left alone with two babies. It was scary at first, but then I noticed how the apartment was getting smaller and smaller. It was like the walls were closing in on me. I felt like there was no oxygen left. I started panicking. There was no way out. I was too afraid to take the babies outside by myself. The first time that happened was when they were about 6 months old. I remember that day when I took the babies by myself. I remember being so proud when I actually stepped foot on the street. We went to the park and had a blast on the swings.

Third recommendation is: do not, I repeat, do not step on that scale. If you are anything like me, you will be curious about your weight, but trust me when I tell you, don't do it. Your hormones are still adjusting. You are in the middle of nowhere, mentally. Don't make it harder on yourself. There will be time, and you will get back in the shape, just give yourself some time. Don't try and do everything at once. One step at a time. Once you give birth, you will be in a state of survival for a while, even if it's just one baby. You will be shocked, but your scale will be shocked too, so just don't do it.

Fourth, very important thing, accept help. Something that me and my husband failed to do. We honestly thought that we would do it all ourselves, but you really can't. Well, actually, you can, because we did it, but it's hard as shit. So just make it a bit easier on yourself, and accept the help from whoever offers. I wish we could go back in time and say "yes." We actually thought that the help will kind of appear out of nowhere from our family, but that didn't happen.

Our families kind of disappeared, which is also what can happen, so keep that in mind. You think you have a strong support system, but then you give birth, and nobody is there. Weird to admit that.

The fifth thing, and probably the most important one, be present with your child. Being present with your child equals being productive. I always thought that I'm supposed to be doing all the things, but being with my children was like the last thing on my list. Your kid will be just fine if all you have to show for the day is cuddling with him. Your kid doesn't care if the dishes are done, and the floors are mopped. All of that comes later. Just be present. Remember, you are the whole world to your child, and that's the most important thing.

I wish I lived by these rules. I wish I had the wisdom to think of all these when I was in the trenches of postpartum. I wish someone had told me these things. There was no one for me, but I'm here for you, so just please, take my advice, and be merry.

***

Motherhood is hard. For many reasons. It's important to remember and accept it. Motherhood is not for everybody and that's okay. The trick is, you will never know if motherhood is for you until you have a child, although, some people know. I feel like only people with children will understand people who never want to have children. You may love your child endlessly, but not love being a mom. It happens, but it's not talked about nearly enough. Because there is shame, there is stigma about it. You "supposed to" love everything, you "supposed to" enjoy everything that has to do with parenting. The truth is, you won't. And that in fact, is totally okay.

In my journey, I honestly enjoy being a mom, but there are parts of it that I enjoy less. Being a mom includes a lot of things, such as cooking, cleaning, doing grocery shopping, and those are some of the things that are less enjoyable. I love playing with my kids, I even have no problem changing their diapers, but all of the little routine things are madly exhausting. Laundry that never ends, dishes that you are constantly doing, dusting, cleaning, washing the floors. Maybe that's why they say that you need financial stability. You can hire a person to clean and cook for you and your family, that makes it so much easier. I wish I had that opportunity. I wish I had this option, to free up my time for my kids, and not constantly think what needs to be done.

My weeks go by pretty fast, because of all the routine things that I have to do on a daily basis. During the newborn stage, I actually couldn't wait until we find our rhythm. I couldn't wait for the "normalcy." Here it is. It is also very tiring. You do everything over and over and over again. Every single week, every single day. The only part that makes everything better is the kids. They learn something new every day and you will be touched by that. All those little milestones that kids are supposed to do, will come unexpectedly. Once day, you wake up and your kid is playing "peek-a-boo" with you, and it warms your heart. You smile and you laugh and you play with your kid, but then... then you supposed to get back to your chores. It sucks. Between the laundry and dishes and all the rest of it, you sneak in a little play time with your kiddos, and you are constantly on the go. It breaks my heart to think about it, because routine gets you tired so fast.

Routine is also important for your kids. Schedule and predictability make your kids aware of what's to come, so they are ready. They are ready to eat, they are ready to play, they are ready for bed. I used to never be a morning person. I watched sunrise maybe twice in my life when I stayed out partying too late. Now I watch sunrise every day, because kids wake up at the ass crack of dawn. I used to never say "good morning," because I hated waking up early, now, it's the first thing that comes out of my mouth. "Good morning my sweethearts!" With a huge smile and so much energy, I greet my babies. And I enjoy it. I love it. You learn to adjust.

No matter how much you enjoy your kids, trust me, you will be waiting for that bed-time routine. The funny thing is that when they are asleep, you will go back to your camera roll and watch the pictures and videos that you took of them that day. Believe me, you will be taking tons and tons of pictures and videos, because you want to remember every little thing. Motherhood, huh? It's one long, wild rollercoaster.

***

Having twins rocked my world, in the best way possible. I was living in my own little bubble, doing my own little things, every day, not giving it a second thought. When I had kids, I realized how small my world actually was. My world has expanded now, and I couldn't be happier about it. I realized that there is so much more to life than just going to work and just living, just hanging out with your friends. All good things, no doubt about it, but a child... A child brings new meaning to your life. A child teaches you so much. My children saved me, now looking back, my children saved my life and filled it with so many different emotions and feelings. I honestly don't know if there is anything else that even comes close to having a child.

Yes, everything is hard. Yes, you're constantly exhausted and tired. Yes, you are sleep deprived and hungry, and you are annoyed at every little thing, but then... Then your little porcupine starts laughing out loud. Then your little baby kangaroo starts crawling. Then your little sweet pea starts walking and clapping and you forget everything. Your heart fills with this sense of purpose and reassurance that maybe you are doing something right. Your heart smiles, like it never smiled before. You start laughing like you never laughed before. Seeing your child make the slightest progress makes you so happy. Everything is new, for the baby, and for you. You grow with them. You learn with them. And you change. You change without even realizing it.

After a while of feeling so lonely, and depressed and exhausted, I finally see the light at the end of the tunnel. I now know that I'm not alone. I will never be alone ever again, because I now have these two amazing humans by my side. This thought makes me smile, and feel warmth and happiness inside. Looking back at everything I went through, it was a great school of life. It was very challenging and the hardest thing that I have ever done, but it's so worth it. I am so excited to see what's next, I am so intrigued to see what comes next. Most importantly, I am ready, and you are also ready. So I guess, my final words would be "just wait." You just wait.

Just wait…
Just wait, until your baby is on your chest.
Just wait, until your baby grabs your finger.
Just wait, for that first smile.
Just wait, for that first coo.
Just wait, when they roll over.
Just wait, until they sit on their own.
Just wait, until they stand.
Just wait, and feel.
Just feel how your heart is full of joy.
Just feel how you are overfilled with love.
Just feel how madly you're in love with them.
Just feel how complete you are.
Just wait, and feel.

If you are struggling, know that you are not alone, and it's not forever. There are more people here for you, than you know. I am opening my line of communication.

Email me: lifeasajokeauthor@gmail.com

Good or bad, doesn't matter. Please reach out.

Helpful resources:

National Maternal Mental Health Hotline:

+1(833)943-5746

National Suicide Prevention Lifeline:

+1(800)273-8255

Postpartum Support International Helpline:

+1(800)944-4773 - postpartum.net

National Nonprofit provider of support, education and research on higher-order multiple births:

www.raisingmultiples.org

Support for families with multiples:

multiplesofamerica.org

In this day and age everyone is on their phones watching videos, and I would like to thank you for picking up a book and dedicating your time to be my reader. A witness to my life. I thank you from the bottom of my heart, for spending your precious time on my book. I appreciate you.

Printed in the USA
CPSIA information can be obtained
at www.ICGtesting.com
CBHW032331181024
16047CB00001B/200

9 798218 490966